THE LEADERSHIP DOJO

THE
LEADERSHIP
DOJO

Build Your Foundation
as an Exemplary Leader

■

Richard Strozzi-Heckler

Foreword by Richard Leider

FROG, LTD.
Berkeley, California

Published by Frog, Ltd.

Frog, Ltd. books are distributed by
North Atlantic Books
P.O. Box 12327
Berkeley, California 94712

Cover and book design by Claudia Smelser
Cover photo: © iStockphoto/jamesbenet
Printed in the United States of America

The Leadership Dojo: Build Your Foundation as an Exemplary Leader is sponsored by the Society for the Study of Native Arts and Sciences, a nonprofit educational corporation whose goals are to develop an educational and crosscultural perspective linking various scientific, social, and artistic fields; to nurture a holistic view of arts, sciences, humanities, and healing; and to publish and distribute literature on the relationship of mind, body, and nature.

North Atlantic Books' publications are available through most bookstores. For further information, call 800-337-2665 or visit our website at www. northatlanticbooks.com. Substantial discounts on bulk quantities are available to corporations, professional associations, and other organizations. For details and discount information, contact our special sales department.

Library of Congress Cataloging-in-Publication Data
Strozzi-Heckler, Richard.
  The leadership dojo : build your foundation as an exemplary leader /
Richard Strozzi-Heckler.
    p. cm.
  ISBN 978-1-58394-201-7
  1. Leadership—Psychological aspects. 2. Self-culture. 3. Moral development.
4. Employee empowerment. 5. Mind and body. 6. Aikido philosophy. I. Title.
  HD57.7.S784 2008
  658.4'092—dc22
                          2007009717

1 2 3 4 5 6 7 8 9 DATA 14 13 12 11 10 09 08 07

*This book is dedicated to Jadon and Chance
and the next generation of leaders*

ACKNOWLEDGMENTS

There is insufficient space here to include the countless people who have contributed to this book. However, I would like to acknowledge and deeply thank the following people who have contributed significantly to this work, this book, and me.

- Maharaj Charan Singh for the spiritual guidance that has sustained me for a lifetime, as well as the spiritual teachings of Dr. Randolph Stone, Chogyam Trungpa Rinpoche, and O Sensei, Morihei Ueshiba.

- Saotome Sensei, Nadeau Sensei, and Doran Sensei for their generous aikido teaching.

- My partners at Lomi School—Robert Hall, Alyssa Hall, and Catherine Flaxman—who were at the beginning of all of this.

- George Leonard and Wendy Palmer, whose partnership at Tamalpais Aikido Dojo is felt and appreciated to this day.

- My old and long-term friends Soto, Tom Lutes, Richard Leider, Dan Petersen, Peter Luzmore, Larry Burback, and

Jasper Redrobe Vassau, who unhesitatingly give me the feedback and laughs that I need.

- Fernando Flores for his rigor and generosity in bringing a new interpretation to language and action, and for trusting me with his clients and colleagues.

- The present and former staff at Strozzi Institute, who make so much possible: Mark Mooney, Alice Christensen, Karen Short, Gail Michelle, Kathleen McCauley-Anast, Anna Scott, Jennifer Lalor, and Kate Slater.

- The many students at Strozzi Institute and Two Rock Aikido, who sincerely committed to the practices of embodied leadership and provided much of my learning.

- General Jim Jones and Sergeant Major Royce Coffee for their vision and service.

- Nancy Hutson, Staci Haines, Sartaj Alag, Ed Perry, Ariana Strozzi-Heckler, Woody Allen, and Peter Luzmore for their advice, guidance, and hard work.

- Richard Grossinger, Lindy Hough, Mark Ouimet, Elizabeth Kennedy, Pam Suwinsky, and the rest of the team at North Atlantic Books who made this book possible.

- My children and grandchildren, who are at the heart of what inspires me: Tiphani, Django, Wesley, Paloma, Jack, Jadon, and Chance, thank you for enriching my life in immeasurable ways.

CONTENTS

Foreword by Richard Leider   xi

Introduction   1

ONE   We Are All Leaders   9

TWO   The Cultivation of the Self   19

THREE The Place of Awakening   37

FOUR   You Are What You Practice   55

FIVE   The Body of a Leader   85

SIX   Leadership Presence   117

       Notes   189

Whenever I give a speech at a business meeting, speakers are often asked to sign a nondisclosure form revealing whether or not there might be a conflict of interest. So, in the spirit of full disclosure, let me say right up front that Richard Strozzi-Heckler is one of my dearest friends and one of the most gifted visionaries I know.

Visionaries in any field have the rare capacity to see our world from a fresh perspective. They also have the ability, often, to put that viewpoint into words so that we, too, can learn to see with new eyes. Richard's viewpoint in this book is to help us see a new world of embodied leadership in action. He sees from the perspective of an aikido teacher with a thirty-year history of practice. He sees from the vantage point of an accomplished clinical psychologist. He sees from the experience of a compassionate and wise elder who has been on the front lines of leadership education for many years.

The wisdom in this book is grounded in real practice. I have had the rare privilege of teaching with Richard in corporate leadership and team programs and have witnessed the breakthrough possibilities available through the somatic practices he teaches. Through our joint work, I have become increasingly clear that information does not change behavior. Practices do. It is clear to me that we must engage the whole leader—mind, emotions, spirit … and body. When we work at that level, leadership development sticks.

Personally, Richard has illuminated the embodied leader in me, as well. I find myself thinking again and again on some of the things he teaches. He has struck some deep chords within me. Here are several of Richard's insights from the book which have found deep resonance within me. They are a sampler of the wealth of truths to be found throughout this book:

~The body we are is the life we live.

~The self is the leader's primary source of power.

~The body is indistinguishable from the self: it is essential to include the body if one wants to build the skills of exemplary leadership.

And what does all this have to do with leadership development? Well, in a highly competitive world, the key to exemplary leadership is first, practice—blending leading from within with leading out there. The ultimate leadership challenge is, indeed, self-leadership. And this book makes a critical contribution to this self-understanding.

Many books come across my reading table each year, but it has been a long time since one of them impressed me so much as this one has. I value Richard's vision and wisdom. And by the time you finish reading this book, ther's a good chance that you will, too.

—Richard J. Leider, Founder, The Inventure Group,
and author of *The Power of Purpose* and *Repacking Your Bags*

I n 1985, after sixteen years of working primarily with individuals, groups, and teaching professionals in a body-oriented psychology, I embarked in a new and unanticipated direction. I was selected to be part of a team that designed and conducted a bold and experimental training for the Army Special Forces. Our task was to increase the physical fitness, mental enhancement, and team cohesion of the Army's Special Forces' soldier. In the words of an officer who promoted the program: "To train a holistic soldier."

For six months our team introduced twenty-five Green Berets to the newest methods of mind/body/spirit integration including aikido, other martial arts, nutrition, physical fitness training, stress reduction, meditation, warrior values, healing arts, team building, and communication skills. Code-named the "Trojan Warrior Project" after the Homeric Greek soldiers who hid inside the belly of a wooden horse, this classified experiment produced positive, off-the-chart results in every area tested.

Even though these men were the most highly trained soldiers in the U.S. Army, through this training they radically improved their existing scores in the areas of physical fitness, mental alertness, team alignment, psychological balance, and moral integrity. The results of the Trojan Warrior Project made it apparent that the research I had been conducting in human performance for nearly two decades with individuals and small groups could be applied to teams and organizations with significant impact.

At the conclusion of the program, when the men returned to their units, a curious phenomenon began to occur. Their commanding officers began reporting that the leadership skills of these men had dramatically improved. This was unexpected in that the curriculum of the Trojan Warrior Project was not specifically designed to address leadership issues but to improve individual and team performance. Soon, the Trojan Warrior Project began to be referred to as a "leadership program" in military circles. Subsequent programs with the Navy Seals and Marine Corps produced similar comments from senior leadership: the practices the participants were doing created significant advances in their ability to lead, motivate, and mobilize their troops. While it made sense to me that the whole of one's life—professional and personal—would be positively affected by the cultivation of mind, body, and spirit, it aroused my curiosity as to why the project produced such positive results in the area of leadership. Soon I began to look more closely at the foundation of exemplary leadership and how it can be developed.

When the project was declassified I published the book *In Search of the Warrior Spirit*, chronicling this training and its impact on individual soldiers and the trainers as well as turning a critical eye on the negative consequences of technology on traditional warrior values. This caught the attention not only of other branches of the military but of the business world as well. The idea of training the whole person, coupled with the skillful action of the warrior, seemed to strike a chord in the business world. Keeping in mind that the book didn't make any claims about leadership, it wasn't long before I was asked to deliver adaptations of the program to the corporate world under the heading of "leadership and management training." This became a rich laboratory for exploring the relationship between leadership and mind/body/spirit training.

I began by asking three questions of every team and organization I worked with. In an initial meeting with forty senior executives at AT&T, for example, I proposed the question, "What does a leader do?" and I received forty different answers. Responses included motivate others, execute plans, manage meetings, delegate responsibility, give orders, design strategies, produce organizational charts, make speeches, inspire, balance the budget, hire the right people, build alliances, mobilize skills, maintain an optimistic mood, and so on, until we had a whiteboard filled with the varied activities that took up an executive's time. This informal poll was duplicated in other companies, and inevitably it was the same: as many different answers as there were people. While all these activities were relevant to leadership, it was clear to me that performing these tasks didn't necessarily make a successful leader. I wanted to know who the person was behind these activities. What ground of being did he or she embody to successfully perform these actions?

My second question, "What are the character values most essential to exemplary leadership?" produced an entirely different response. The answers fell into a consistent and predictable pattern. Whether the poll was taken with Chilean telecommunication executives, the senior leadership of the Marine Corps, thirty-something technology entrepreneurs, European financiers, directors of nonprofits, U.S. Senators, CEOs of Fortune 100 companies, or Canadian utilities executives, the same virtues unfailing appeared. Honesty, account-ability, integrity, vision, commitment, empathy, courage, trustwor-thiness, and self-control showed up time and again as the hallmarks of a leader. The literature and research on the character aspects of leadership also reflected this response. There seemed to be a universal consensus about the type of character values necessary for leadership and for leading an honorable life. Moreover, this list of values was hardly new. As far back as Plato and Thucydides in the West, and the Indian epic *Bhagavad Gita* and Buddhist text *Abidharma* in the East, these attributes have long been distin-guished as the cornerstones of exemplary leadership and life. It seems that as long as human beings have recorded their history there has been universal agreement about what kind of person is a successful leader.

When I asked my final question, "How do you teach these vir-tues?" I was met with blank stares. It seemed I had reached the end of the trail. Most managers and leaders could say very little about how the character values of leadership are learned, and even among the brightest, the conversation descended into clichés: "It's either there or it isn't"; "You can lead a horse to water but you can't make him drink"; "Leaders are born not made." Presumably, this has something to do with the difficulty of measuring values, and business schools are notorious for demanding empirical measure-ments for everything. A typical refrain in the business world is, "If it can't be measured, don't manage it." Nonetheless, the point is we can give examples of a leader's behavior but nothing about how it's learned. Bookstores are filled with stories of great leaders and what they did in certain situations, but nothing about how they got there. There's precious little written about the *how* of leadership and certainly no notable discourse representing it. It's as if we know what we're aiming for, and we know when it's present, but we don't know how to get there.

This book is about learning the human side of leadership. It's informed by a lifelong passion for learning and more than three decades of studying how people excel and achieve mastery. This hasn't been an academic pursuit of poring over texts but working closely with leaders and leaders-to-be in a wide variety of organizations. This includes the senior leadership of the Marine Corps (including the Commandant and Assistant Commandant), the command staff of the Special Operations Command, Navy Admirals, a multitude of executives from large multinational corporations such as AT&T, Microsoft, Citibank, Pfizer, British Petroleum, Cisco, Hewlett-Packard, Cemex, and American Express; and national utilities, nonprofits, and small technological start-ups in the United States, Canada, the United Kingdom, Europe, Asia, and Latin America. Working in these different environments, I realized that leadership is something that can be learned, and it's generated in relationship with others. Exemplary leadership is not a thing—the correct genes, an appointment, a technique, or the chance of the draw that favors one individual over another. Exemplary leadership is a way of being, whether you're leading others or leading your own life. Leadership *can* be developed; it's a choice and an option. It's a skill and art that can be developed through commitment and practice. Leadership is about living our purpose while engaging deeply with others. The Leadership Dojo is a place, an operational distinction, a community, and a set of practices that produces exemplary leaders. In the Leadership Dojo, leaders and managers learn to embody and live their full potential.

This book does not present a theory of leadership, a list of what leaders do, or a leadership style. While it's intended to be a thoroughly practical approach to leadership, it is neither a manual nor a recipe book that delivers tips and techniques for leadership in "ten easy lessons." Conversations about leadership tend to lean toward the banal: "Leadership is needed now more than ever"; the situation is further aggravated by applying the monthly fads and trends of the "expert." The world doesn't need another book of leadership slogans.

What is offered here are the practices and sensibility of the requisites that make leadership possible, authentic, and ultimately practical. By *requisites* I mean the underlying structures necessary for one to fully embody the qualities of exemplary leadership. Throughout this book I refer to *exemplary leadership;* by this I mean the ability to organize and mobilize the talents and skills of others (or yourself) toward an observable result. This is accomplished through pragmatic wisdom, grounded compassion, and skillful action.

I claim that this underlying structure positively affects all the activities of a leader. By *underlying structures,* I mean the living body that is the storehouse of 3 billion years of wisdom, intelligence, and experience. Moreover, we say that through certain practices this bodily wisdom is accessible to everyone. As the periodic table of elements has remained essential for understanding our physical world for generations, the principles in this book will remain a ground for training leadership over time. While I present a number of principles, examples, and practices, the fundamental and recurring notion is that living fully in our bodies is the essential ingredient for leadership—leading others and leading our lives.

If this idea seems perplexing, rest easy; it is explored and harvested in every chapter of this book. In fact, this is a book about the Body of a Leader.

In looking at what it means to train the requisite skills of leadership, we examine:

- Why leadership? in Chapter One
- The cultivation of the self in leadership in Chapter Two
- The "Dojo" or training environment for leadership in Chapter Three:
  - Learning for action
  - Practice
  - Fellow learners
  - Teacher or coach
- How practice develops exemplary leaders in Chapter Four
- The Body of a Leader in Chapter Five
- A Leadership Presence (the requisites for exemplary leadership) in Chapter Six:
  - Centering
  - Facing
  - Extending
  - Entering
  - Blending

ONE

We Are All Leaders

Leadership and learning are indispensable
to each other.

John F. Kennedy

■ ■ ■

On a recent trip to Tanzania, I had the opportunity to walk
with a small band of Hadza, a hunter-gatherer tribe who
live a preagricultural existence, as their ancestors did a
hundred thousand years ago. The Hadza have virtually no material possessions and they live a nomadic existence. Moving lightly
across the African landscape, they rarely spend more than ten days
in one spot as they follow migratory routes and the weather in their
search for food. They forage for berries, roots, tubers, and honey,
all the while keen-eyed for the game they shoot with poison-tipped
arrows. They live uncomplicated lives in a direct relationship with
the natural world.

One morning as we walked a wooded ridge, one of the men

pointed out a small gnarled bush and initiated an animated conversation between the men and women. After some discussion the women began to dig around the root system for the nutritious tubers it produces. While the women broke the ground with digging sticks, the men smoked and engaged in conversation, occasionally kibitzing and offering suggestions to the women's efforts. At one point, as the women were seated in the three-foot hole they had dug, pulling at the thick tubers, one of the members of our group jokingly remarked to the men, "I see you let the women do all the hard work." Unaware of the implied humor of the Western notion of equal rights, a Hadza male replied in a serious tone, "No, we all learn how to do everything. Everybody's a leader. If something happened to her we have to know how to do this, or we'd die."

"Everybody's a leader. We all learn how to do everything."

The idea seemed to ricochet off the blistering African sky. The light brightened and the world expanded while everything in it became more lucid. I looked at our small group: educated, well-informed, decent, upper-middle-class professionals who, by the standards of the larger world, had achieved considerable success in their lives. They had all become successful leaders by focusing their energies into one field, achieving expertise by narrowing themselves into a specific, well-defined career. As specialists they had become efficient in a single activity. While specific technical achievements had been won, along with a marketable identity, the greater view that included meaning and purpose had been lost. In many ways that's why we were in East Africa: to see how others lived, to see how else to lead our lives and learn new ways of leading.

I looked at the Hadza: they could do many things well. They were all generalists, some more talented at some things than others, but they could easily interchange roles. They all knew how to find water, make tools, skin an animal, care for children, stalk a gazelle, create a fire with a stick, pass on their oral tradition, find medicine in the forest, lead ceremonies, build a shelter, engage in diplomacy with other tribes, sit quietly, walk long distances. If one of them suddenly died, someone would immediately be able to step in and get the job done. Their social order would be intact and the survivability of the band would be minimally impacted. They were all leaders. In their case, community unity and a sustainable lifestyle had been achieved; meaning and purpose were alive and vital; scientific achievement was nonexistent.

I do not romanticize the Hadza. I am not a Luddite, nor do I hanker after a time in the distant past of my own culture. I take a stand for community, connection, fulfillment, the full expression of our calling, and the health of our minds, bodies, and spirits. I tell this story because it makes us consider leadership anew and it points to a cost that we pay for an increasingly specialized, technologically oriented way of life, a way of life that began with the Industrial Revolution and has radically accelerated in the age of information. We begin the twenty-first century dominated by a technological culture that, with remarkably few exceptions, has created social and economic institutions that treat people as instrumental means, slotted into roles that wed them to machines. We live in a time where very few seem able to answer with any depth the question, "What are we striving for?" We live in a world that increasingly lacks any firm grounding in meaning, values, or purpose. The result of this numbing and isolation is a staggering cost to the human spirit.

These are leadership concerns.

Consider these statistics from Northwestern Mutual Life, the American Institute of Stress, the American Psychological Association, and the National Institute for Occupational Safety and Health:[1]

- Disabling stress has doubled since 1990.

- Between 70 percent and 90 percent of employee hospital visits are linked to stress.

- Depression has doubled with every generation since the 1920s.

- More than one million people per day are absent from work due to stress-related disorders.

- One in three Americans seriously thought about quitting work in 2000 because of job stress, and one in three expects to "burn out" on the job in the near future.

- A landmark twenty-year study conducted by the University of London concluded that unmanaged reactions to stress were a more dangerous risk factor for cancer and heart disease than either cigarette smoking or high-cholesterol foods.

- The American Medical Association reports that 75 percent of physician visits are psychosomatic.

- Employee stress costs business $300 billion per year in absenteeism, loss of talented employees, health costs, and programs to reduce stress.

- The cause of the majority of employees' stress and lack of emotional commitment are the very managers who are supposed to be leading them.

- The American Heart Association says that one-third of the American workforce now has high blood pressure.

- In their book, *Follow This Path,* Coffman and Gonzalez-Molina report that "more than forty-two independent Gallup studies indicate that approximately 75 percent of employees in most companies are not engaged in work ... and disengaged employees cost companies hundreds of millions of dollars annually." They go on to say that their research shows that "employees don't leave companies. They leave managers and supervisors whom they feel don't care about them either as individuals or as employees." And "providing appropriate emotionally skilled leadership can impact the U.S. economy to the tune of $254 to $363 billion annually."

If this isn't enough, a recent Gallup poll that canvassed more than a billion people in sixty countries revealed that four out of five people said they were dissatisfied at work because they didn't think they could bring all of themselves to their job. A similar poll by *USA Today* corroborated these figures when it reported that only 20 percent (one in five) of all working Americans said they get up each morning looking forward to going to work.

As stunning as these statistics are, it doesn't surprise us, because it speaks directly to our own lives and to those of the people around us. These figures confront us on two fronts: the significant loss of productivity, innovation, and creativity at the workplace, and the overwhelming amount of sickness and despair that so many people experience as a result of spending more than a third of their life in activities that have little or no meaning to them and with leaders who think of them as machines. More than ever we lead lives of ease and luxury, yet fewer and fewer individuals can claim that what they are doing produces fulfillment and satisfaction.

Looming in the background of these statistics is the question of leadership: Where is our leadership in regard to these issues of purpose, meaning, productivity, and valuing people and their well-being? How are we training our emerging leaders? How do we lead our own lives?

Leadership is one of the most enduring of universal human concerns. Since the beginning of civilization, leaders and leadership have been written about, extolled, criticized, and debated. But for all of its controversy, the necessity for exemplary leadership is always present.

Every age and culture makes its own unique case for leadership, and this is equally true for ours. The explosion of technology in the past twenty years, the increasing awareness that people are the key factor in organizational success, machines steadily taking over routine work, the percentage of knowledge workers growing, and organizations developing both economic and social agendas all require that more individuals, despite their roles, step into leadership positions.

Everyone needs to be a leader.

Moreover the deterioration of the natural environment, the increase of the international arms race, the erosion of public education, the breakdown of the family, and social anomie and fragmentation argue against traditional hierarchical leadership. No one is so naïve today to think of today's leaders as the all-powerful, all-knowing speakers of truths, ensconced on the top floor.

Arguably the quality of life in the twenty-first century will have everything to do with our quality of leadership; and whether we like it or not, all of us are increasingly being asked to take leadership roles in our lives. What we need is a renewed vision, a new interpretation of learning, and a training of leaders that produces commitment, passion, values-centered action, and a centered presence.

The test of contemporary leadership is to attend to the force of history, act fully in the present, and build narratives and practices for a generative future. This is the exemplary leader who embodies grounded compassion, skillful action, and pragmatic wisdom.

CATEGORIES OF LEADERSHIP

Leadership can be divided into two categories: leadership as a role and leadership as a way of being. The principles of the Leadership Dojo address *both* of these groups: those who are leading others and those who are leading their own lives.

Leadership as a role is the category with which we are most familiar. Beginning with hunter-gatherer bands, through agrarian societies, and expanded upon in the Industrial Revolution there is a historical record of individuals called upon to formally lead others. In contemporary life, this is the individual who is a leader within an organizational setting. This includes the private, public, military, government, and social spheres. The roles can be chief executive officer of a corporation, chairperson of a board, manager of a team or division, director of a nonprofit, military leader, PTA president, business owner, project leader, or community organizer.

The second category of leadership—*leadership as a way of being*, which is more of a modern phenomenon—consists of those individuals who are leading their own lives. At more than thirty-five million, independent contractors in the United States (a group considerably larger than those working for the federal government) represent a sizeable and growing population. More and more people are realizing that their companies are not going to take care of their futures, and it's necessary for them to take charge of their lives. These are the growing legions of small business owners, coaches, consultants, facilitators, mediators, trainers, artists, teachers, craftspeople, and writers.

What is required of today's leader? We can group the capabilities of modern leadership into three broad categories:

1 Intelligence

2 Technical skills and knowledge of his or her industry

3 Being a particular kind of person or self

Intelligence. Today's leader has to have a certain level of intelligence. Intellectual might is necessary in order to think through complex issues, navigate through a wide range of commitments, hold multiple horizons of time, manage a diversity of people, analyze data, and think both tactically and strategically.

Technical skills and knowledge of his or her industry. Technical skills such as accounting, analyzing reports, business planning, running a division, strategy, financial implementation, and so forth are necessary skills for leaders. It's also necessary for a leader to be sufficiently knowledgeable in his or her area to be successful, whether it's finance, manufacturing, pharmaceuticals, advertising, marketing, technology, health care, raising children, or running a dairy.

Being a particular kind of self. The focus of the Leadership Dojo is the development of the virtues, character, and ethical and moral values that make up the exemplary leader. I call this the "Cultivation of the Self." In the Leadership Dojo, the premise is that the "self" is the leader's primary source of power. Clearly, intellectual capacity and specific technical skills matter, but alone they do not make a powerful leader. It's the self that is able to mobilize and motivate others, coordinate effectively with them, build trust, and generate positive moods. We have seen time and time again that the value one has as a person, that is, the self that one is, ultimately becomes the deciding factor in success as an exemplary leader. In Chapter Two we examine what it means to cultivate the self in leadership. And remember, we mean both leaders who lead others and those who lead their own lives with meaning and purpose.

TWO

The Cultivation of the Self

Leadership has nothing to do with power and
rank but is a matter of self-realization; attain
self-realization and the whole world is found in
the self. Leadership has nothing to do with wealth
and status, but is a matter of harmony.

Lao Tzu

■ ■ ■

A defining moment in my life arrived in the form of a teacher.
It was at a time when I was living in a general un-
settledness and I was looking for a new direction. I was
visiting a friend, a respected practitioner of the Chinese martial and
healing arts whom I hadn't seen for a while, and in the course of
our conversation he suggested there was somebody I should meet.
In his own mysterious way he didn't say why I should meet this individual, but I trusted him and said yes. The next day he called and
said he had arranged a meeting the following week.

On the scheduled day I arrived early and waited at a café with an outdoor sitting area. I positioned myself so I could see the front entrance of the building where we were to meet and also be visible to my friend when he arrived. At this hour there was no one on the streets and I sat with a cup of hot tea, enjoying the muscular clouds that glided effortlessly through the spring sky. There was little I expected, yet I was curious about what would unfold.

At some point my eye caught a movement on the alley side of the building. Two men stepped out of a back entrance, and after they conferred momentarily, one went back in and the other walked slowly in my direction. There was nothing exceptional about him, either in dress or looks, except that he moved with an implacable air of gravity. Not solemnity, but with a purposeful ease that informed his entire being. He was slight in build, but his presence seemed to fill the alley. As he came closer I could see that he was taking everything in, as if the alley were a museum and all the debris held some indeterminate value in his eyes. I felt that I was also in his field of vision, although he never looked directly at me or acknowledged me. At one point he picked up a wooden slat that had broken off a packing crate and began to move in elaborate, circular movements—sometimes broad and sweeping, other times fast and collected—carving the air with it. There was nothing forced or staged about what he was doing; the movements were seemingly done for their own pleasure. His grace and poise cloaked an immense internal power.

As he continued to move in my direction, I could see his authority was generated from an inner axis that emanated openness while being solidly contained. He radiated warmth, but manifested cool. I found him easy to look at, as if he were cut from a single cloth; there was nothing frivolous or wasted about him. As he approached the end of the alley he looked up and down the street with a disposition of unflappable pleasure, as if he were a pilgrim who after an arduous journey had finally arrived at a holy site. He looked at me and smiled, his face lit like a lantern. He then turned and walked back down the alley and entered the building through the side door. I was transfixed by the power of his presence, and it moved me to find out who he was.

The power of that extended moment, nearly thirty-five years ago, carved an image into my consciousness of what I can only call the human possibility. It was simply someone walking through a vacant alley with a discarded piece of wood, yet what was revealed to me were the virtues of presence, power, focus, balance, integrity, grace, and a wholehearted commitment to living each moment fully. What was inexplicable was there was no exchange between us or established relationship upon which these assessments could be based. Yet there was a way that this man comported himself, his living presence, that spoke to me about who he was as a person. This was the individual that my friend wanted me to meet, and in the three decades that I've known him his ethical and moral behavior have been consistent with the presence I observed that day.

I tell this story because it speaks to a fundamental claim of the Leadership Dojo: the self is the fundamental power of a leader and the self is indistinguishable from the body. That is, our comportment, body alignment and function, capacity for action, and how we presence ourselves through our bodies reflects who we are as persons, reflects our orientation to others and to the world. In other words, the body is a manifestation of a person's philosophy. The embodied self is the primary source of power for a leader, and it can be trained through practices.

Powerful leaders embody a centered presence. This centered presence mobilizes and motivates people to action. It calls forth their talents and skills; it increases trust and fellowship. The relaxed alertness that results is utterly compelling. I'm calling attention to the relationship between moral power and how we live in our bodies. As an example, consider this description of George Washington when he was the Commanding General of the Continental Army. The following account from a diary occurs during a visit in 1778 to a hospital at West Point.

> The appearance of our Commander in Chief is that of the perfect gentleman and the accomplished warrior. He is remarkably tall, full six feet, erect, and well proportioned. The strength and proportion of his joints and muscles appear to be commensurate with the pre-eminent power of his mind. The serenity of his countenance, and majestic gracefulness of his deportment, impart a strong impression of that dignity and grandeur, which are his peculiar characteristics, and no one can stand in his presence without feeling the ascendancy of his mind, and associating with his countenance the idea of wisdom, philanthropy, magnanimity, and patriotism. There is a fine symmetry in the features of his face indicative of a benign and dignified spirit.... He displays a native gravity, but devoid of all appearance of ostentation.[1]

The diarist says he relates this full account as it "serves to remind us how much his mere appearance among his scattered brigades meant in preserving morale and how much he *embodied* [italics mine], quite literally, the Continental Army." It is important to note that the observer, a junior officer, had no other acquaintance with General Washington other than being with him as he moved through the hospital at West Point. His conclusions were not based on a long relationship or any conversations whatsoever. He drew ethical and character conclusions about Washington only through his comportment and the way he presenced himself. Reading the biographies of Washington, one quickly sees that these are the same traits that he began developing as a youth and were evidenced when he was President. In other words, the observations of the diarist were consistent with the Washington that we know in depth. Again, I'm drawing attention to the way in which we comport ourselves; our embodied presence is inextricably linked to who we are ethically, morally, and spiritually.

We are accustomed to think of someone's character as either a prominent behavior pattern or what they say is their purpose and intentions. But if we look at those times of crisis when we are called upon to act ethically and morally, what is observable is a dynamic unification of mind, body, and spirit—a presence—that acts with dignity, directness, and decisiveness. A grounded and passionate ethical and moral stand is inevitably generated from a body that is both internally calm and outwardly prepared for action. It is relaxed without being slack and strong without being stiff. This is the self that can effectively move into powerful decisive action or take a position of dignified restraint. When Thomas Jefferson said that Washington seated himself better upon a horse than anyone of his time, he is not reflecting idly on Washington's equestrian abilities.[2] He's framing the potency of the connection between an authentic centered presence and moral and ethical authority. He's suggesting that by observing how a person sits on a horse—or, I would add, walks, engages in an unfamiliar situation, or rakes the lawn, for example—it's possible to assess that person's power, restraint, balance, and capacity to act, to listen, and to commit. By observing how one is in her body, we can tell a great deal about who she is as a person. This is reminiscent of Arnold Palmer's comment, "I can tell everything I need to know about a person by watching them play eighteen holes of golf."

The point of view I'm suggesting here requires us to reconsider the common interpretation of the self as the exaggerated development of a single part of our personality, perhaps at the expense of the other parts. Or the Cartesian perspective that separates mind, body, and emotions, which inevitably positions character as what a person says. Instead a more useful interpretation is to see the self as a quality of being that reflects one's wholeness. Furthermore it grounds the notion that the self is indistinguishable from how we present and express ourselves through the body.

At this point it's vitally important to understand that the development of a Leadership Presence, through the cultivation of the self, is not to be confused with self-esteem training, personality development, or self-improvement seminars. I say this because the centuries-old tradition of self-mastery—the rigorous struggle to transform our limitations into strengths and to invigorate our virtues into skillful action—that leads to a deep authenticity and service to others has been infantilized into the quick-fix, self-improvement industry of the twentieth century. This movement, with its attendant obsessions of material gain, superficiality, and narcissism that Walt Whitman called "The Great American experiment of Me," has made it fashionable to dismiss, out of hand, the path of self-mastery in business, military, and government because it has come to represent something soft, or airy-fairy, in the public eye. This cynicism has created a critical void in leadership training, a void that is reflected in the cost of our humanity, health, and ability to bring out the best in others and ourselves.

Leaders cultivate the self in order to better serve others.

There is a long and rich tradition that goes back thousands of years in both the East and the West that spells out a path of self-mastery that is designed *to serve the greater good.* This is not a path of self-aggrandizement, but one in which we grow and transform ourselves in order to contribute to a vision larger than our petty desires. Consider Plato speaking more than two centuries ago: "We will be better and braver if we engage and inquire than if we indulge in the idle fancy that we already know or that it is of no use seeking to know what we do not know."

In the path of self-cultivation, the emphasis is not concerned with "getting better," fixing oneself, or indulging one's ego, but performing with mastery. Self-esteem training concerns itself with producing positive self-regard. This is a process through which one feels better about oneself, which is important, but it may not necessarily lead to new actions or improved performance. It's also a slippery slope in that "self-feeling" can easily be disconnected from service to others. The leadership path of self-cultivation is concerned with developing leaders who embody the ethics of individual responsibility, social commitment, and a moral and spiritual vision. It's a rigorous discipline that has its roots in two ancient traditions from the East and the West.

In the Western tradition, Aristotle, in *Rhetoric*, speaks of *ethos*, a type of leadership that is "a form of influence that causes other people to change their values and so their performance of tasks."

He goes on to explain that ethos is a leadership virtue distinct from rhetoric or persuasive language. Ethos is not what a person says or promises, but it's her way of being in the world, a presence and comportment that effects others to follow her and to be open to her ideas. Here the words of William Shakespeare come to mind: "By my actions, teach my mind." Ethos implies that the fundamental and distinguishing elements of an individual's character, as observed in the person's countenance, has the power to mobilize and change another's outlook and performance. When someone is the embodiment of ethos, those around him act with purpose and conviction. Ethos is not simply an intellectual principle of character, but a living body presence. As Eric Fromm said, "Ideas do not influence (men) deeply when they are only taught as ideas and thoughts.... But, ideas do have an effect (on men) if the idea is lived by the one who teaches it; if it is personified by the teacher, if the idea appears in the flesh."[3]

In this state a person has the courage to take a stand for what she cares about as well as the flexibility to adapt to a changing world. It is the opposite of *pathos,* which arouses one's pity and sympathy. Ethos arouses respect, mobilization, and action.

In the Eastern tradition, *shugyo* consists of two Chinese characters, "to master" and a "practice." Literally, then, it means to "master a practice." In everyday language, however, it is understood as self-cultivation. In this tradition the goal is to discipline one's spirit, or character, by using one's body. In a general sense the activity is not what is important; we could include walking, running, yoga, swimming, or golf as the practice. It is the intention behind the practice that produces the meaning. Shugyo, or self-cultivation, carries the meaning of developing the human spirit through physical practices. This is not to be mistaken for the modern Western sports goal of developing the motor skills and coordination of the body while ignoring the power of mind/body/spirit synchronization. Shugyo has the goal of achieving a level of maturity that generates positive emotional states and controls negative ones. This is a different end than the sports objective of strengthening the body so that it can successfully perform certain movements.[4]

The practices of shugyo are designed so that the personal self will ultimately be absorbed into the world self. While this may sound vague and fuzzy, it simply means that it is a leadership virtue to master one's personal wishes, cravings, and desires *for the sake of* a larger commitment. Shugyo reflects the importance of going beyond the appetite of the self-centered ego if one wishes to gain mastery, live an exemplary life, and lead people. In this state the body is relaxed, the mind is free of self-conscious thoughts of success or failure, and one's energy or intention flows freely, without obstruction. There is a balance between pushing forward and retreating. From this centered presence one can act directly and appropriately to take care of the situation at hand. This state of body-mind synchronization is more effective than the personal, centralized self. The culmination of shugyo is pragmatic wisdom, skillful action, and grounded compassion—a self that is not driven by compulsion, fear, or self-interest, but acts for the greater good.

Our bodies will determine our behaviors.

The following story exemplifies how cultivating the self produces a leadership sensibility that contributes to the success of the individual and the entire enterprise.

Jerry is the CEO of a successful technology company that he

founded ten years ago. He received his M.B.A. from a prestigious university, and before starting his own business he was the senior vice president of a Fortune 100 company. His traditional business credentials are impeccable and his direct reports jokingly call him "Patton" for his energy and hard-driving approach. For the first seven years Jerry's company thrived and grew at an average rate of 15 percent a year. He was on the fast track to bringing his company public when a sudden downturn in the economy produced a decline in sales, and then a long stall affected profits and morale. He tried to "fix" this downturn by increasing his autocratic command-and-control style of leading. Some of his best talent began to leave, the company downsized, and it became questionable whether it would survive.

Jerry was known among his employees as overcontrolling and confrontational. He had lost a few key people because of his volatility; those who stayed had compensated either by avoiding him or numbing themselves during his outbreaks. These traits had remained more in the background when business was good; Jerry would adopt an overly cheery, smiley-face demeanor that made his employees equally uncomfortable. When the company ran into trouble, his aggressiveness escalated and, in the words of one his managers, "He responded to the increased pressure by turning up the volume and turning down the listening. He became more demanding and harsh. This alienated people in the company and our customers began to see him as needy and desperate. Everyone kept away from him." Jerry felt that the antidote to the company's downturn was for everyone to work harder and longer. As his aggressiveness took on a relentless edge, the exodus from the company intensified.

Jerry saw the problem as outside of himself, something that technology or a systems change could solve. He was looking for tips and techniques to fix his management and sales teams. "Perhaps," he commented, "we need a new marketing strategy." When I told him it was necessary that he first examine his leadership style, he was taken back. It had never occurred to him that he might be part of the problem. "Look at my history of success," he said. "Why do I need to change?"

Jerry lived in a world in which people were seen as pieces to be moved on a gigantic chessboard and the importance of camaraderie, joy, and team esprit were irrelevant. His business acumen, intelligence, the marketplace, and his hard-driving style had allowed him to succeed up to this point; it hadn't been necessary for him to engage firsthand in the fundamental human issues of coordination, dignity, listening, mood, trust, authenticity, and purpose. But he was now at a crossroads that required him to transform his leadership style ... or fail. He was initially exasperated to think that he had to be self-reflective, to see that the way he shaped himself in an aggressive and dismissive way alienated others, and how his over-bound, overcharged style limited the way he listened to both his staff and his customers. But it was as if he had backed himself into a corner, and it became apparent that his "take no prisoners" style of leadership was the core of the company's problems. Jerry was plenty smart, had the know-how within his industry, but he failed miserably at collaborating, building trust, or motivating others.

There were three phases in my work with Jerry and his team. In the first phase I worked with Jerry one on one and then with his entire team. In the beginning of our work, Jerry thought he would take a number of personality tests and instruments like Myers-

Briggs and we would analyze them and that would change something. He was surprised when I said I would have him experience
his body, the shape of his living and leadership, and see what that
told him. I pointed out what I saw in the way he organized himself
bodily and I asked him to experience this from the inside. This gave
him a firsthand awareness of his comportment and presentation
to others. This new awareness opened up new choices for him. In
addition he committed to certain practices that began to shift the
way he comported himself and therefore the way he moved and
interacted with the world.

Jerry had an overdeveloped, overbound upper body that was
set on a pair of spindly, thin legs. His toes were clawlike, his arches
and feet pulled away from the ground like a bird clutching a teeter-
ing wire. His chest was stiff and immobile, held high and puffed
out as if he were holding his breath. His shoulders were pulled up
and inseparable from his neck, which constricted his throat and
voice. This gave the impression of an inverted pyramid with his
weight held high and very little support from underneath. When he
walked he looked like he was stumbling forward, forcing himself to
move and keep up with himself, always off-balance. He did this by
squeezing the muscles in his pelvis and buttocks and throwing his
rigid frame forward. There was a conflict in his body between moving ahead and restraining himself. He was like a sausage, tied off
on both ends, his excitement bouncing around in his chest cavity,
where he was emotionally suffocating.

Over time Jerry disclosed that his father had died when he was
young and his mother separated herself emotionally from him and
his older brother and withdrew into alcohol. He remembers trying to keep up with his older brother and forcing himself to walk

prematurely to keep up with him. He pushed himself to appear older than he was and at the same time he longed for the comfort and nurturing support of his mother. He had learned to anesthetize himself so as not to feel the unmet longing and at the same time to reflexively push himself forward in order to belong. This conflict in muscle groups became a physical rigidity and produced a narrow emotional range. He must not let go of control, yet he must move forward. His woodenness allowed very little to come in and it allowed very little to get out. He was like a kid, secretly in need of support and encouragement, but imitating his version of manhood—a hybrid of John Wayne and the Terminator.

As our work deepened, he spoke about feelings of inadequacy even though he presented to the world as arrogant, overbearing, and authoritarian. "Always," he told me, "I have this feeling of having to be in control. I have to keep myself and things moving ahead, yet I'm constantly unsure about doing the right thing." He saw that by holding his breath he could overcome the sensations of fear and he could then move forward on his stiff legs. While he longed for support, he inhibited it by his shallow breath pattern and rigid torso. This stiffening of the muscles around the ribcage, the heart, and lungs gave others the impression that he was above it all, a better-than-others attitude. This style of self-organization alleviated his anxiety but it produced mistrust and resentment in others. Jerry simply steamrolled over people without feeling, thinking, or blinking. He charged ahead by numbing himself to his sensations and feelings, and therefore to the feelings of others. His fear of collapse created his compulsive need to be the smartest, most assertive, the one always in charge.

Through this process Jerry saw three important things about his style of leadership. First he saw that his bodily structure was intimately linked with who he was as a person and therefore as a leader. This led him to see that to shift himself, to change his behaviors, it was necessary to shift the shape and motility of his body. Second he saw that despite what he was feeling or thinking, there was a way he comported himself that produced mistrust and resentment. In this he saw that it was possible through certain practices to produce a different presence, one that made people want to be around him, trust him, and be motivated by him. This wasn't simply acting in an inauthentic way to appear in a better light, but a way of being that began from the inside and flowed outward. Finally he saw that the self in leadership was as important, if not more important, than how smart you are or how technically competent. This opened him to seeing people as possibilities, as partners instead of instrumental means, and as collaborators instead of minions to dominate.

As Jerry shifted his behavior, we began working with his team. We began by looking at how they shaped themselves (how they organized themselves bodily) individually and as a team. Initially we started with exercises in which their historical way of being in the world, as individuals and as a team, were revealed to them. This illuminated the different patterns, both positive and negative, that they automatically fell into with each other. By observing themselves from this perspective, they were able to become less reactive to each other and more accepting of their individual strengths and limitations. They could see what traits were useful to them and what were simply conditioned responses that no longer had value for their business. They learned this by interacting physically together in practices appropriated from *aikido*, a Japanese martial art.

This type of somatic practice is more powerful and effective than taking a standardized personality test, as it allows one to literally feel and directly experience one's own patterns of behavior and conditioned tendencies. One's embodied history then is not simply an intellectual idea but something that is felt and lived. There existed choice where before there was only unexamined reaction. This developed trust with each other, out of which more effective collaboration and cooperation practices were implemented. The exercises that revealed these tendencies were not necessarily "heavy" psychological insights but were revealed as a way of being that was reflexive and automatic. Members of the team began to lighten up with each other and respectfully note when one of them fell into these conditioned patterns.

Jerry was now able to see how he created a mood of resentment and resignation within the company; he and his team also saw how their automatic reactions affected the way they related to customers and the marketplace itself. It became obvious that Jerry's personal style had become a company style, and it hindered the way management saw business opportunities. The company culture was to see people as objects that were to be moved around, run over, or dismissed—not as multidimensional, living beings who held possibility for partnership. The employees saw how many of their recent failures had to do with how they mismanaged their relationships with customers and how they had missed possibilities in the global marketplace. In a lighthearted moment someone called Jerry the "the Tonka truck" when he fell into a shouting fit. Jerry laughed and from then on he was referred to as "Tonka" when he flew off the handle.

In the second phase we implemented relational practices and

processes that were necessary for the staff to succeed at the individual, team, and company levels. This included structured conversations that ranged from intimate conversations about personal style and history to strategic business conversations. We engaged in movement practices that increased their capacity for coordination in business processes. They learned to be direct and courageous with each other in a way that enhanced both their dignity and success as a team. We taught them how to receive and deliver assessments that produced action and collaboration. It's important to note that these conversational practices were not simply following a script or reading a "how-to" book. The team members practiced speaking to each other from a centered presence in which they learned to pay attention to mood, dignity, listening, competency, and capacity. Trust deepened between them, and the intimacy that followed made it possible for them to strategize and innovate in ways they never thought possible.

In the third phase they engaged in practices of reading and anticipating the world. This allowed them to perceive each other, their customers, and their marketplace from a fresh perspective. They investigated marginal discourses that challenged their traditional belief systems; they had conversations with people who could articulate the historical forces that were shaping the world; and they engaged in movement practices to shape an identity that would produce success in a fast-moving world. Building on the foundation of trust and cooperation they had developed in the previous two phases, they were able to speculate, collaborate, and innovate in new ways. This kept their thinking vital and their capacity to move in the marketplace agile and flexible.

During my work with Jerry, he learned how to manage his moods and he became a more effective listener to his employees and customers. He was able to recruit and retain bright, ambitious new people. His management team learned processes that allowed them to coordinate and collaborate more powerfully together. The company turned around and once again became a leader in its field. During this same period of time, the company added new technology and became active in Internet commerce, but Jerry's report, as well as that of his colleagues, was that the company's success couldn't have happened without the change in him and his team.

The practices of the Leadership Dojo produced several leadership skills in Jerry and in the culture of his company.

- A Leadership Presence of integrity and authenticity
- The capacity to:
  - generate and manage moods that are coherent with a productive and balanced life
  - cultivate, manage, and repair trust
  - coordinate effectively with others
  - motivate and mobilize others
  - stay emotionally balanced in times of adversity and change
  - listen deeply, moving skillfully with other's concerns
- The importance of being a lifelong learner

These skills of leadership may seem obvious to the point of being elementary. Certainly they are not novel or contestable among what are commonly seen as the necessary social skills for a leader. Yet it is rare to be in an environment that promotes practices that develop these skills. The Leadership Dojo addresses how this knowledge is translated into performance.

In Chapter Three we look at the elements of the Leadership Dojo.

THREE

The Place of Awakening

If you want one year of prosperity, grow grain.

If you want ten years of prosperity, grow trees.

If you want one hundred years of prosperity,

grow people.

Chinese proverb

■ ■ ■

magine this: On a whim you stop by to visit a friend, but just as you arrive he's walking out the door. He's on his way to a professional seminar that's associated with his work, and he invites you along. He's an executive at a large corporation, so you presume this seminar will have something to do with management techniques, corporate strategy, or running a division. On the way there you imagine, as one does when suddenly faced with a new future, what it will be like to be at his class. In your mind's eye you see rows of chairs lined up in a large room, with the teacher or professor behind a lectern, a large screen behind her for PowerPoint presentations, and a whiteboard nearby. You imagine yourself sitting quietly with your friend and the other students as the teacher lectures while her main points are projected on the screen. Everyone is taking notes; perhaps some of the students have laptops in which they type the ideas. At the conclusion of the lecture there's a question-and-answer period. The mental picture you've formed seems typical of what would happen in a classroom situation. This makes you feel secure and mildly curious about what you will learn in your friend's class.

When you walk through the door of the classroom, your sense of what is about to occur immediately vanishes. The classroom is a large, open space with chairs around the edge. Though the room is expansive and airy, it also conveys a feeling of warmth. There's an ambience of both scope and intimacy. There are fresh flowers on a small table at the front of the room. The curtains around the windows are open and the natural light from outside brightens the entire space. Flip charts taped on the walls refer to the points to be covered. Computers and notebooks are on the chairs, but no one has one in hand. In fact no one looks prepared to take any notes at all or to sit in the customary rows in front of a lectern. Your friend tells you where you can sit and says that he will check in with you at the first break. He doesn't seem surprised by the seemingly unusual arrangement of the room. He goes out into the open space with the other students who have formed a half-circle around the teacher.

The teacher speaks about how the practices they will soon engage in will generate an effective style of leadership. By *effective* she means an executive presence, the skill of listening to others, being centered in chaos and uncertainty, building trust, and acting decisively. She demonstrates an exercise with an assistant and explains what to look for when practicing the exercise and how to orient these practices of leadership to the students' business concerns. In the demonstration the teacher and the assistant move together, sometimes vigorously, sometime barely touching; at times they even grab each other. As they physically interact, they speak to each other in ways that correspond to the movements. For example, when the teacher grabs the assistant by the arm she says, "We need to talk about the way you're dealing with customers." Or, "You need to step up to the plate and fulfill on your commitments."

She explains that grabbing her assistant's arm in this manner will evoke an ingrained conditioned tendency of how he reacts to pressure. This reactionary tendency will be the same in the workplace as in this practice. This is so because the reactive tendency lives within our nervous system, and our nervous system exists where we are. Through this practice, she explains, her training partner will become intimately acquainted with this automatic reaction. By becoming aware of his reaction pattern, he can choose to return to center instead of being a victim to it. To demonstrate the point, the assistant straightens and relaxes from his initial angry, defensive stance, turns toward the teacher, and says in a collected, direct manner, "What do we need to do to get back on track?"

The teacher then points out that the "grabber," as a leader, is practicing the appropriate amount of pressure needed to get the person's attention. Too much pressure and the person feels mistreated and not taken care of; not enough pressure and he doesn't feel there's a commitment from the "grabber." The teacher explains that, of course, we don't physically grab people at work, but we are grabbed by a look, a tone, a particular stance, even a request or assessment. She claims that by practicing in this way we will become more in harmony with those with whom we interact on a daily basis.

You can see a coherency between what they're saying and what their bodies are doing. The teacher uses further examples to help the students understand the point of the practice, and then the students pair up and practice what was demonstrated.

The teacher and assistant move from pair to pair making comments, working individually with people, fine-tuning movements and phrases, and in general encouraging the students in their exploration of an effective Leadership Presence. There is a relaxed, friendly atmosphere in the room and at the same time a mood of rigor and discipline. People are having fun while they're learning; an air of commitment permeates the interactions of the students. There's aliveness in the room that's compelling. You wonder what it would be like to be out there with them. It's a bit intimidating because the practice requires a straightforward and direct relationship with your partner and you're not sure how you might do. There's a requirement to be present in a genuine way and express who you are and what you care about. At the same time, there is a mood of openness that promotes authenticity and encourages learning.

The teacher calls everyone together for a discussion about the learning and to address any questions. People describe what they're learning about the phenomenon of leadership, values, presence, and commitments in their professional lives. The teacher continually orients the conversation to what is relevant and practical, and she encourages everyone to take part in the conversation. A feeling of curiosity and speculation dominates the discussion. It's like a laboratory where everyone is organized around a set of foundational principles, and inside of that they have the liberty to experiment and innovate. Sometimes the teacher encourages the speaker to go deeper and other times she elaborates on a point that someone makes, or she might just acknowledge the point and go to someone else.

She then demonstrates the next exercise, what to pay attention to, and how it's relevant to leadership. Everyone takes a new partner and they again begin practicing in earnest. The pattern of practice, discussion and questions, practice, and changing partners occurs a number of times. It's a highly interactive environment in which everyone adds to the conversation and then takes the new principles into practice. At the end of class there is a review of what was presented and then a debriefing about the learning. The teacher speaks about what to pay attention to and what to practice until the next meeting. She gives general guidelines for everyone; for a few, she offers additional assessments and instruction. Everyone completes the program by stating their commitments and their moods. As the students move toward the door, they are animated and engaged with each other; they seem optimistic and challenged.

On the way home you find yourself somewhat at a loss about how to reply when your friend asks about your evening. It's so completely different than what you expected or imagined that you're still sorting it out. You're not sure if you've learned anything about business in the conventional sense, but it is clear that during the course of the class many of the students took on a different quality of being that made them appear more powerful, trustworthy, and committed. It also occurs to you that by virtue of practicing the different principles taught in the class they would be able to handle the pressures of their business more effectively while generating a positive, can-do attitude. And without knowing anything more about them, you would be inclined to be on their team or have them on your team. Simply, they were people you could trust, learn from, work with, and would like to be around. But most important, you see how this kind of training could help you become better at what you do.

This scenario is a description of the Leadership Dojo. The concept of the dojo as a place to learn leadership is the cornerstone of this book. We now look more closely at the history of dojo learning and what it means to learn in the Leadership Dojo.

THE LEARNING ENVIRONMENT OF THE LEADERSHIP DOJO

The term *dojo* derives from the traditional Japanese arts; it means the "place of training." Its origin is from the Sanskrit word *bodhimanda,* which translates to the "place of awakening." A dojo, then, is a place to awaken to and learn new ways of being in the world. It is remarkable to think that as long as human beings have recorded their history—for more than 5,000 years—there are references to places of gathering together to learn and to "wake up." The idea of coming together to learn and embody universal principles of leadership is not a new or marginal one. The dojo is an ancient tradition that addresses the concern for self-mastery, learning, sustainability, and innovation. When the uninitiated sarcastically regard this learning as the "soft" skills of leadership, they quite perfectly confirm their ignorance about a centuries-old practice that exists solely to produce mastery in a chosen discipline.

42

The concept of *Do*, which translates literally as "Way," sheds some light on what is meant by training in a dojo. The *kanji* or ideogram for *Do* is composed of two parts. One part depicts a man walking on a road. The other is the human throat, which surrounds the jugular vein, representing the very core and pulse of life. This image represents a person walking toward life. In other words, a "Way" is a theme of engagement and action, nothing short of a commitment to a fully lived life. The dojo is a place where we align with our purpose, cultivate the self, learn new skills, and unite with the spirit through rigorous and self-generative practices. This is what it means to be "on a Path of Awakening."

In traditional Japanese culture there are many kinds of dojos: martial arts dojos, flower-arranging dojos, *sumi* painting dojos, meditation dojos, tea ceremony dojos, for example. In these dojos, students practice a specific art together under the direction of a qualified teacher. While the students learn and gain competency in a discourse or craft, they also build the foundation for a moral, ethical, and spiritual life. As they learn their particular art or skill they will, over a period of time, also come to embody the fundamental skills of personal mastery, social dignity, and service to a greater good.

In Japanese these two elements are expressed as *ri* and *li*. *Ri* is universal principles and *li* is skill acquisition. These are spoken of metaphorically as the two wheels of the cart; both wheels are needed to move the cart forward. To learn only one element leaves the individual imbalanced and ineffective. In the Leadership Dojo, one learns the principles of embodied leadership, *and* becomes competent in the specific skills needed in one's enterprise.

The tradition of learning both specific skills and fundamental principles can be seen in the martial arts dojos of eighteenth- and nineteenth-century Japan, where the Japanese Samurai honed the art of warfare *(budo)* in order to protect their communities and resources while at the same time building a code of ethics *(bushido)* for living a meaningful life. While they learned the specific skills of war fighting—sword, jiu jitsu, archery, spear, battlefield tactics, and such—they learned a warrior's presence, ethics, code, and morality. Furthermore, these competencies and virtues came to maturity through recurrent practices, not academic learning. In other words, it wasn't assumed that the sensibility and skills necessary to be a warrior could be casually absorbed through the culture. What was required was a place where one could rigorously learn and train with competent teachers and other dedicated students working toward a common goal. I offer this historical precedent as a way of illustrating that the Leadership Dojo, as a place of learning, includes a multiplicity of concerns, from the specific skills required to fulfill professional commitments such as sales, management, product development, strategic thinking, and marketing to the more ontological skills of meaning, presence, purpose, vision, building trust, communication, coordination with others, and culture.

I stepped into my first dojo when I was twelve years old. It was comprised of a mat about the size of a large living room in a corner of a drafty Navy airplane hangar. A small vase with a flower and a scroll of Japanese calligraphy served as the head of the dojo. My mother had enrolled me in the class because of disciplinary problems I was having at school. A Navy family, we moved frequently, and as the new kid in class I responded to the taunts and pushes by pushing back. I increasingly became more involved in fights on the playground. A vice principal suggested I enroll in judo as a way to put discipline in my life and probably to make his life easier. My mother vigorously objected, thinking it would only teach me how to fight better, but he waved off her protests and assured her that it would be the right thing for me. I was simply grateful that my father was at sea, rendering him unavailable to deliver his own reckoning for my delinquent ways.

The moment I entered the dojo, all the concerns about fighting, discipline, mother, and father instantly faded away. We bowed reverently toward the small table that held the calligraphy, then to the teacher and our training partners, and then we proceeded to systematically and joyfully slam each other to the mat. It was a rare mixture of fierceness, discipline, and just plain fun. The teacher skillfully kept our raging adolescent hormones at the edge of mayhem, allowing us to test our strength without damaging anyone, including ourselves. I instinctively knew this was a place that I could learn about the relationship between power and responsibility. "What is too much force, what is too little force, and what is appropriate" was the litany when you had someone in a chokehold and felt the pulse of life under your fingers. To stray too far from this sensibility would cause harm and mistrust.

Leaders need to daily face the lessons of what is too much and what is too little with those they lead.

Since that time many decades ago I have trained at innumerable dojos. Some were so elegantly crafted and detailed as to belong in a museum. Others were garages, converted barns, drafty gymnasiums, churches, storefronts in strip malls, YMCAs, and I fondly remember one that was laid out in the corner of a small park in the middle of a large city. What is important to remember is that the structural elements of wood, plaster, and bricks that would constitute acceptable architecture do not make a dojo. The objects and materials that make up a dojo have meaning only in relationship to the story we have about them. A dojo is a space of commitment in which people engage in a collective practice for learning and transformation. I have a friend who acknowledges that any place he has learned in is a dojo. This has included conference rooms, restaurants, park benches, a friend's home, a hospice, even a jail cell where, as a lawyer, he had to interview a client. My teacher once tapped me on the chest and said, "Here is the dojo." He was reminding me that ultimately the dojo lives in our hearts and minds. The dojo exists because of the meaning we give it. This meaning can never be lost from its place in the world because it *is* that place. Simply, the dojo is where and what we declare it to be. Each moment can be a place of awakening, of training, of learning, of walking toward life.

Leaders look for the opportunity to declare the dojo space in which they can learn and help mentor and coach those who follow them.

The world of martial arts revealed to me early on that what I could do was far more important than what I knew or said I knew. Action, in other words, was the virtue, and it spoke more loudly and eloquently than being "head smart." In the martial arts dojo, when someone would speak about how good they were at a particular technique it was only a matter of time before someone would stand up and say, "Okay, let's see what you can do." This was an invitation for the speaker (or braggart) to stand up and demonstrate his claims with an observable result. This is what we called "putting it on the mat." That is, demonstrating you could walk your talk. This wasn't a dogmatic preference for a world of black and white, void of nuance, because there is plenty of that in the martial arts, but rather a realistic concern for what works.

Exemplary leaders do more than talk a good game. Their presence and actions back what comes out of their mouths.

When I was studying aikido in Japan in the mid-1970s it was common for the *gaijin*, the non-Japanese, to meet at a coffee shop or noodle stall at the end of the day to debrief our training. Once in a heated conversation with a group of martial artists from around the world about the merits of one style against another, a fellow student from New Guinea said, "In my country we say that knowledge is only a rumor until it's in the muscle." Everyone fell silent. Our testosterone-driven sense of competitiveness was quieted, and humbled, by the wisdom of what he said. It was one of those crystalline moments when nothing else had to be said. Leadership is about taking skillful action, producing results, and mobilizing others, not simply acquiring academic knowledge.

We learn through our bodies, through recurrent practices, and learning means being able to take new actions. Leadership is a learnable skill.

Trained in the rationalistic tradition, where we are predisposed to think of learning as something that happens in the mind, the idea that we learn through our bodies is somewhat startling at first. We can see the influence of rationalism in our formal education when we recall sitting at our desks reading books, listening to lectures, and reviewing case studies and theories. The body was simply the delivery system that transported us to the classroom and then remained in the background as we absorbed information. This model says someone has learned something if they can understand, analyze, and report back data. This person, we would say, is smart because he or she can prove what they say is true. While this is one interpretation of learning, there is another that has been widely neglected because of the authority of the rationalistic approach. There has been, for example, little recognition given to someone who could produce value through the way they manage mood, how they skillfully coordinate with others to achieve a desired goal, or their ability to ignite the passion and purpose of others.

Once we grasp this rationalistic interpretation of knowledge and learning, we see its imprint in the intimate corners of our everyday lives, as well as in our local and national institutions. As the most prestigious and persuasive model for reality, rationalism accounts for nearly all of the scientific and technological achievements of Western culture. Scientific reductionism, an outcome of a rationalistic philosophy, has made it possible to build bridges, advance medicine, build and fly planes, and expand global communications. Producing extraordinary advances in our quality of life, rationalism has also come at a price. Freely applied to humans, culture, nature, and social policies, rationalistic thinking has stunted our emotional and spiritual literacy.

With our educational institutions now firmly grounded in mathematical thinking, instrumental reason, and pseudo-scientific approaches, we equate the human body with a machine and thinking with a computer. We employ reason and logic to determine our relationship with nature and with each other. We are so firmly entrenched in this way of seeing that our social scientists, economists, and world leaders have become indecisive and hesitant in taking action because of a concern that pragmatic application, regardless of how successful, won't match established theory. Theory has become more important than action, domination more crucial than cooperation, and ideas regarded more favorably than relationships.

Because this model of education has historically produced tremendous success in science and technology, we understandably consider learning to be about accumulating knowledge. This way of learning has its place, but we have become imbalanced and have forgotten the primacy of relationships and how to listen to the wisdom that resides below discursive thought. When people were at the same job, working with the same machine, over a lifetime, this way of learning was satisfactory. This is no longer the case. Not only is there too much information for any of us to process, we are moving at a velocity that demands grounded action instead of theoretical knowledge. We are now at a historical transition in which it is crucial that learning be placed in the context of action, as a way of being in the world, instead of simply being intellectually smart. We challenge the notion that cognitive understanding produces the ability to take effective action.

This way of looking at the world has separated us from our bodies and therefore from our emotions, moods, and our capacity to feel and sense. In turn this has caused tremendous breakdowns in our professional creativity and personal fulfillment. Arguably the greatest cost of the specialization of technological life—and out of which all other damages are birthed—is our separation from the practical and enriching sense of ourselves as embodied beings. Alienated from the wisdom of the body, our lives have become theoretical and abstract, distancing us from the direct, felt sense of living. Our bodies have become sick, joyless, incapable of satisfaction, ineffective in action, and victim to the purveyors of cosmetics, medicine, and the illusion of perpetual youth. Except as delivery mechanisms that haul our brains from meeting to meeting, our bodies have grown inconsequential. This willingness to abuse our bodies is the genesis of abusing other bodies. To solve the many dilemmas we now face, it's important to have leaders who take action from their hearts and guts as well as their minds.

We have become afflicted by a cultural amnesia in which we have failed to remember that we're a unified constellation of sensations, images, stories, emotions, meaning, and feelings that are contained within the biological framework we call "body." We are not machines; we are organic, feeling, multidimensional beings who are not simply extras in some corporate extravaganza. If one of the effects of an information-based society is to turn us away from the reality of the bodily life, the numbers cited in Chapter One about our declining health and well-being will only increase. This alienation from our bodies and the fragmentation it produces in modern life—as evidenced by the billion-dollar industries created by antidepressants, antacids, anxiety relievers, migraine medication, and flights to virtual worlds—suggest a lack of vision in our leadership and our personal inability to lead our own personal and professional lives.

Unlike our conventional educational system in which we sit and take notes during a lecture, learning in the Leadership Dojo is characterized by placing our bodies, over and over again, in learning practices. In the dojo the teacher declares the subject being taught, speaks to what concerns it addresses in the world, reveals it in action for the students, and then the students practice. The focus is on the practices and the coaching of the teacher. This is radically different than sitting passively and listening to a lecture or studying charts and diagrams. Learning is possible in a lecture hall, but it's academic knowledge, not embodied knowledge.

Academic knowledge is an intellectual understanding; it fills the head with information. This has its place in certain domains, but in the domain of leadership it is not always relevant. Embodied knowledge, on the other hand, is the skill to act appropriately at the appropriate time. It is immediate, available, and responsive.

Academic knowledge does not live in the present moment; it is stored in theories, books, and computer chips. Embodied knowledge occurs through recurrent practices with the body, not with memorization or rote learning.

This is not an argument against theoretical learning; it's declaring that learning in the Leadership Dojo leads to the capacity to take new actions as a leader.

While the emphasis in the Leadership Dojo is building the skills for exemplary leadership and team enhancement, there are also principles structured into this learning environment that can form the internal culture of an organization. These principles become the ethics of the company, or ways of doing business with internal and external customers. These principles are the integrity between speech and action (telling the truth to customers and colleagues) and foster proper respect and obligation to the teacher (customer, boss), to fellow students (colleagues), and to the dojo (workplace) itself. Principles permit leaders to synchronize mind and body (making and fulfilling commitments), honor tradition (business processes) while they stay open to innovation, take a stand for a position without arrogance or aggression, make a lifelong commitment to learning, and maintain the proper equilibrium between self-gain (career) and the concerns of the community (corporate vision). These principles are always present when training in the Leadership Dojo and inform the background ethics, morals, and norms of the company.

Exemplary leaders understand the importance of learning and learning organizations. We have the possibility of learning throughout our lives, and this can happen inside our organizations as well. The capacity to learn helps us to move our professional goals forward and to evolve as people. In a world of continuous change and constant social innovation, learning has taken on a new importance. Where it was once sufficient to be competent at the same job over a lifetime, we are now required to continually learn new skills, to adapt to people with widely different backgrounds, and to be flexible enough to change roles, job positions, and organizational directions many times in our careers. Learning over the course of our lives has become a necessity, but even more critical is learning *how* to learn. To become competent in the "how" of learning increases our effectiveness as well as enhancing our general wellbeing. Learning how to learn is one of the most powerful ways of dealing with the changes of today's world. When we understand the fundamentals of learning we are able to adapt, change, and take new actions in a much more timely fashion. In this time of accelerated change, learning to learn gives us a competitive advantage. To succeed in the future it is necessary to be learning individuals in learning organizations. The Leadership Dojo is an environment in which we learn not only specific social skills necessary for exemplary leadership, but also *how* we learn.

Practices

- Have you ever been in a dojo? (Remember this doesn't refer to martial arts.) What did you learn in this dojo?

- What dojo(s) do you belong to now? What are you learning in this dojo(s)?

- What is the cost of not being in a dojo?

- As a leader, is there a place that you declare a dojo?

- Is there a place that is necessary for you to have a dojo or "dojo conversation" in your role as leader or in your life? What value would it produce?

- What value do you see in having a teacher, mentor, coach, or guide?

- As a leader, what is the value of being part of a dojo?

In Chapter Four we look more in depth at the principle of practice in the Leadership Dojo.

You Are What You Practice

We are what we repeatedly do.

Aristotle

■ ■ ■

In the mid-1950s an up-and-coming sportscaster named Howard Cosell interviewed Carl Furillo, the right fielder for the Brooklyn Dodgers. Cosell began the interview by describing Furillo in glowing terms as the master of the right field at Ebbets Field, the Dodger home stadium. The right field at Ebbets, with the odd angles of the outfield wall, was notorious for its difficulty to play.

With obvious reverence for the older and well-known Furillo, Cosell asked, "This is such a difficult fence to play, Carl. No one else can even come close to playing it as well as you can. How did you ever learn to do it?"

Furillo looked at him strangely, shrugged his shoulders, and replied as if he were speaking to an idiot, "I friggin' practiced!"

The message is clear: To get good at something, it's necessary to practice.

Carl Furillo knew that his expertise was hard earned. It wasn't magic, a gift from the gods, good luck, or wishful thinking that made him the baseball player that he was. As an all-star veteran who was out on the field every day the answer was easy: practice.

Compare this with a recent ad on television that promotes weight loss with the promise that "you don't have to change your life, you only have to take a pill." We live in a culture that sells the quick fix, instant gratification, and get it all right now, on a daily basis. While we may understand, at least intellectually, the importance of practice when we casually comment to our children that it's necessary to practice when learning to play the piano, type, write in cursive, or drive a car, it's largely an idea that's unexamined, especially in the domain of leadership.

The media and entertainment industries create the illusion that by simply stepping into the right car, dressing in the latest fashions, or dyeing our hair a certain color, our goals will be instantly attained. The idea of committing to a practice to achieve mastery or personal fulfillment is not a highly endorsed idea. When we're continually fed a diet of "fast, temporary relief," there's very little incentive to consider a practice as a way to positively take charge of our health, behaviors, relationships, attitude, or overall success in life, to say nothing of developing leaders.

The notions we do have of practice are from the realm of sports or the performing arts, where perhaps we've had some experience, or at least enough familiarity (mostly as fans), to know that practice is a requirement for success. We hear it in the well-worn joke about the couple who arrive in New York City from Florida and, finding themselves lost in the Lower East Side, ask the first cab driver they see, "How do you get to Carnegie Hall?" (This can be changed to Yankee Stadium, the Metropolitan Museum of Art, or Madison Square Garden.)

"Practice!" the cabbie shouts back.

Yes, we understand that athletes and performers practice, but what is invisible to us is how much they practice. They continue to practice during the entire season, during the off-season, and even while they're in a championship series or in a heavily booked performance cycle. On a recent Ellen DeGeneres show, you could hear the audible gasp of the primarily adolescent female audience as Britney Spears reported that it's not uncommon for her to practice her singing and dance moves twelve hours a day; her life is a continuous cycle of practice, performance, practice. Even when "I'm performing," she said, "I'm all about rehearsing my songs and dances." The young female audience's fantasy about being "the next Britney" if they have the right hairstyle and can perform a few snappy turns in front of the mirror was suddenly shattered.[1]

Larry Byrd, the veteran all-star player for the Boston Celtics, would faithfully go to the arena two hours before every game, whether it was at home or away, regular season or playoffs, and walk the court and practice his shots alone. Sometimes he would sit in the stands and see if he could make a basket from there. When the Celtics won the 1986 championship after a grueling season and playoffs, reporters asked him what he planned to do next and he replied, "I've still got some things I want to work on. I'll start my off-season training next week. Two hours a day, with at least a hundred free throws."[2] Michael Jordan, at the top of his game when he was called the greatest basketball player the game has ever known, would reputedly be the first at practice and one of the last to leave.

Athletes practice three times as much as they play, and the ratio is even higher for performing artists. All this confirms the old martial arts story that defines the master as the one who stays on the mat longer than anyone else. When I'm asked by a student how long it will take to learn a new skill or a new way of being, I'll often quote how military jumpmasters reply to the question, "How long do I have to pull the ripcord of my parachute?"

"The rest of your life," is the jumpmaster's answer.

We have this moment to practice, and we can commit to a lifelong practice.

Furthermore, if we heard a baseball player say, "I'm not going to batting practice anymore, I've already done that," or a heart surgeon who said it wasn't necessary to practice his craft anymore, it would sound ridiculous to us. Interviews with athletes who have just won a game during a championship series will inevitably say it's important to continue to practice the basics, and the losers of that game will inevitably say they need to get back to basics. It would sound preposterous for them to say they didn't need to practice anymore or they had already practiced the basics and they wanted something else to practice. Master musicians speak about how they still practice their scales, award-winning actors regularly practice vocal phrasings, internationally renowned ballerinas still work on *pliés*.

Every time I train or teach aikido I still practice *tenkan*, a turning movement and the very first technique I learned thirty-five years ago. Because I may have gained competency in the movement over three decades of training doesn't mean I abandon it. To begin with, it keeps the movement sharp and fully embodied, which is important because it's fundamental to the art; second, and perhaps most important, is who I am in the movement changes because of the practice. When I say "who I am" in the movement, I'm referring to how I'm observing myself, others, and the environment; that is, how my awareness has grown and therefore expanded my choices, and how my will and skill have been strengthened to enact those choices.

Zen Roshi Richard Baker said it in the simplest of terms when he commented, "Enlightenment is an accident, but practice makes you accident-prone."

If we want to introduce new leadership behaviors in our lives, it's necessary to practice. We also know that to achieve mastery it's necessary to go beyond our comfort zone. (Researchers say 300 repetitions produce body memory, which is the ability to enact the correct movement, technique, or conversation by memory. It's also been pointed out that 3,000 repetitions creates embodiment, which is not having to think about doing the activity—it's simply part of who we are.) Humans will engage in a practice if they're passionate about what they are practicing. We are passionate about what we practice if it's relevant to the life we want to create.

Exemplary leaders are passionate about creating life-affirming futures.

Practice is formalized in sports and the performance arts; why not in leadership, in business, in government?

THE FUNDAMENTAL POWER OF PRACTICES

There are three different types of practices that are important for developing a Leadership Presence:

1 Partner practices in the Leadership Dojo
2 Daily personal practice
3 Practices in the workplace or home

As an example of how someone would engage in these different types of practices to develop his or her Leadership Presence, let me tell you about a woman I'll call Sylvia. Sylvia was a star in the mergers and acquisitions of a large international financial institution. Over the years she had gained a well-earned reputation as a skilled, hard-nosed negotiator who brought significant revenues and satisfied customers into the bank. Sylvia was also known for her tireless efforts and uncompromising approach to doing business, both with herself and her staff. While she was an inflexible taskmaster, she was also known to be fair and generously reward those who earned it.

Because of her consistent success she was offered the directorship of the department, which required an entirely different set of skills than what she was accustomed to employing. Historically, she had worked alone or with a few assistants and now she had to lead and manage the entire department. Her competency was in negotiating financial deals, not in leading and managing others. One of the things missing in her new role was her capacity to build trusting relationships with her colleagues and staff, listen deeply to them, and create a high-functioning team. *Directorship* to her meant dictatorship. She was well meaning and a decent person, but she had no background whatsoever in dealing with people, as was required in this new position. She could make people money, but she didn't know how to lead them.

From the beginning her direct reports balked at her command-and-control style. Morale sagged, resentment increased, and she received failing marks from her team and associates. The question was whether she should return to being an individual performer in mergers and acquisitions, where she had a stellar track record, or invest in her own development as an executive. She sincerely wanted the position, her boss believed in her, but it was clear she had to increase her social intelligence to build an effective team.

The practices of the Leadership Dojo are designed to support the commitments of the participants; therefore Sylvia first had to declare her commitments, what she wanted to accomplish. We have multiple commitments in our life and in multiple domains: health, career, job, spirituality, money, family, relationship, and so forth; but Sylvia was asked to choose a single commitment and work with it. In doing so, she would not only fulfill her commitment but also learn the process of how to fulfill commitments, which she could then apply to all future commitments.

Sylvia's declaration as a leader was to be a more effective listener. She then formed her conditions of satisfaction, or criteria for success, for this declaration. The conditions of satisfaction grounded her declaration in observable results. This is also referred to as a *performance index, deliverables, metrics, benchmarks,* or *criteria* for success.

There are three elements in the conditions of satisfaction:

1 Time

2 Customer or committed listener

3 Observable results

Time is the deadline by when Sylvia becomes a more effective listener. Sylvia said that in a month she would demonstrate progress and at the end of three months she expected to be seen as a different listener.

The *customer* or *committed listener* is someone who would observe the improvement in Sylvia's listening skills and be able to say whether she was improving, or not. This is the person who ultimately would say they were satisfied or not with her progress. In this case it was the senior vice president, Sylvia's boss.

The *observable results* of her commitment, or what it would actually look like, were in her words: "I won't interrupt my managers when they're speaking. All my direct reports will say that I listen to their concerns more clearly and cycle time will increase 20 percent. My team will trust me more, thus making us more effective in taking action."

Practice

- Declare a commitment that you want to fulfill. Speak it in this way: "I am a commitment to . . ."

- Write your conditions of success, including time, customer or committed listener, and conditions of satisfaction.

- Ask your customer or committed listener for feedback about how you speak your commitment. Are you believable to them and do they think your commitment is appropriate?

- What do you notice as you make your commitment? What is easy? What is a struggle?

- What do you notice in your body? Where do you tighten and contract? Are you able to return to center?

- What is your mood after this practice?

Partner Practices in the Leadership Dojo

From a centered stance, Sylvia would stand in front a partner and speak her declaration: "I am a commitment to being a more effective listener."

We ask people to say, "I am a commitment to . . ." instead of "I'm committed to . . ." as a reminder that we *are* the commitment, we strive to *embody* its value and contribution, and we're fully *accountable* for its outcome. The commitment lives inside us and moves out from our center.

After speaking her commitment, she received feedback from her partner, who reported that Sylvia's eyes darted back and forth when she spoke; she also said her breath was high and rapid and that she spoke quickly. Her partner told her it produced the impression that Sylvia was rushing, as if she were racing against time. This matched Sylvia's style of always hurrying, being impatient with others, and never having time for those she managed.

In the next go-around, Sylvia paid closer attention to what was occurring in her body, particularly in her eyes and breath, as she spoke her declaration. She noticed she felt anxious, not really confident of herself, and when this happened she would speed up, as if to override the sensations of anxiety. She then took more time to center herself, made contact with her partner, and let her voice emerge deeper from her belly. As she continued to practice in this way, Sylvia began to relax into herself and into her commitment. Her partners commented that she seemed more authentic, more connected to them and her commitment.

The feedback was not only useful for Sylvia; it was a practice through which the assessors could polish *their* listening skills so they could offer feedback that was actionable for Sylvia. This required that the assessors reflect on certain questions:

- What makes Sylvia credible and what diminishes her credibility?
- Is she persuasive and if so, why?
- What do I see and sense in her presence that makes me want to follow her, or not?
- Is there integrity between her physical comportment and what she's saying?
- Do I want to build a future with her? If so, why; if not, why not?

These are all questions that sharpen one's somatic observation skills, an indispensable skill for leaders.

This practice of delivering and receiving assessments, or giving and receiving feedback, is a necessary skill for leaders and a fundamental aspect of the Leadership Dojo. As I've said before, the Leadership Dojo revolves around engaging in practices with others, not simply digesting lectures or watching slide presentations. The Leadership Dojo is a highly interactive environment in which students learn how to skillfully interact with others while building their leadership skills. Training to receive and deliver assessments in an authentic, direct, and respectful manner with fellow learners exemplifies this type of learning. This practice teaches a level of contact that is personally fulfilling and accelerates one's learning and level of performance. Because it's difficult to truly see ourselves, there's immeasurable value in having competent fellow learners give us feedback about our strengths and liabilities. At the same time it's powerful to embody the skill of making assessments so we can help others to learn and grow.

Learning to give and ask for assessments in the dojo requires a high level of engagement, openness, and commitment—the same conditions necessary to thrive at work and home. In the Leadership Dojo, we emphasize the qualities of appreciation, curiosity, goodwill toward others, and a centered presence when delivering assessments for action and engagement. The assessments are shared in a mood of assisting others to learn, grow, and take new actions. We learn to listen compassionately and to speak directly. In other words, to listen and observe with empathy and respect, but also to speak truthfully when assessing others.

When it was Sylvia's turn to give feedback to her partner, it helped her develop her listening skills, in the service of her declaration. By paying attention to her fellow learners, Sylvia learned what it meant to slow down and simply be with the other person, to let them know that she was present with them without rushing or enforcing her agenda. She saw that by being with her team in this way, she not only built trust with them, she also gave assessments that helped move them toward fulfilling their goals. This practice builds unity among an existing team as it makes visible and operationalizes the team member's commitment to help her teammates, and it raises the standard of leadership for the entire team.

Sylvia engaged in other practices that also helped put her declaration "into the muscle." Sylvia's partner would ask her about her commitment while she slowly placed her hand on Sylvia's chest. The partner, also practicing being centered, did this as a literal and figurative way of asking Sylvia to be present for the conversation. Sylvia instantly responded by leaning forward, pushing against her partner's hand, which again was consistent with her forward, hard-driving style. But when her partner suddenly released her hand, Sylvia tipped forward off balance.

Working with her body in this way, Sylvia came to see how ineffectively she managed her energy, always exerting too much force for what the situation required, and how she would lose contact with the person in front of her. She connected to how this pattern created distrustful and unproductive relationships, and how it tired her out. She saw that if she connected with the person in front of her by paying attention to the contact of their hand on her chest, she was less of a victim to her automatic reaction of pushing forward. By paying attention to her body, she could clearly gauge how to somatically organize her energy so that the pressure actually helped her center, and she became more present to herself, her partner, and the environment.

Her partner then asked, with her hand extending on Sylvia's chest, "Why is this important to you?" (referring to her commitment) and then, "How do you know you'll be successful if you fulfill on this commitment [conditions of satisfaction]?" Predictably, Sylvia went into her head, lost contact with her partner, and began her uncompromising press forward. Being able to see this conditioned automatic response much more quickly now, she also returned to center more quickly. She changed roles with her partner, centered, and asked the same questions of her partner. In this role Sylvia began to see that over time her listening skills were beginning to sharpen.

In another practice, two partners faced Sylvia with their arms extended, hands lightly touching, palms facing her, forming a waist-high gate or barrier. She stood five paces in front of them, centered, and spoke her declaration. She then walked through the "gate" of hands in front of her. For Sylvia the gate represented the" obstacle" of her inner voices saying she didn't have the ability or will to change. True to her style, she leaned forward and barged through the gate, using more force than needed. When she received this feedback from her partners, Sylvia reported that as she approached the gate she compensated for the negative inner voices by going faster and trying even harder. Yes, she managed to go through the gates, but by using far more energy than was necessary; and her brusqueness alienated her partners.

After receiving this feedback, she returned to the practice and went through the gate again with a heightened awareness that translated into a more centered presence. Because choice follows awareness, this gave her more choice over her automatic hard-driving, tipped-forward style. In subsequent turns, she was more balanced, more powerful, and more in contact with her partners. She would also be a gate for her partners as they practiced embodying their declarations. This was valuable for her in that it again included her commitment of listening, as she would somatically pay attention to the other person and then give them feedback.

An example of another practice in the Leadership Dojo is the *rondori. Rondori* is a Japanese word that roughly translates "chaotic movement." In the martial tradition there's a rondori at the end of every black belt test. A rondori occurs when the examiner calls out multiple attackers to rush the candidate at the conclusion of a grueling hour-and-a-half-plus examination. Many years ago, as an examiner for a series of black belt tests in aikido, I realized that this is what the many individuals and teams that I worked with were going through in their personal and professional lives. In other words, they were required to deal with multiple concerns, one thing coming right after another throughout their day. Of course the concerns weren't people physically trying to attack them, but they were verbal attacks, requests, assessments, disagreements, faxes, breakdowns in communication, conflicts, phone calls, and so on. You get the point; this is probably very much like your life and the lives of those around you.

In the rondori at the Leadership Dojo, the student comes into the middle of a large circle of her fellow learners, centers, and speaks her declaration. Then one after another the students form the circle around her and walk toward her at a fast pace, one hand outstretched toward her chest. She then moves among them, slipping past them, turning them, and walking with them—a variety of moves—while she centers on her commitment. Often there may be as many as four or five people at once in the middle of the circle coming at her (competing for her attention, as in her everyday leadership role). Inevitably she gets bumped, jostled, and thrown off center while being coached by the teacher and her fellow students to center and hold her commitment.

When Sylvia began her rondori, it was clear that she was someone who could act decisively and with authority. She moved with power and intention; her movements were centered and precise. She handled the situation with confidence and poise. But when she was jostled and thrown off balance, which normally happens to everyone in the rondori, as it does in everyday life, she stiffened and became harsh, her actions abrupt and severe. In her effort to recover, she aggressively pushed forward and adopted a slash-and-burn, intimidating style, insensitive to the people who came toward her. Her fellow learners soon became cautious and protective as they entered the circle, fearful that they might get "handled" if they got too close.

These practices with an existing team increase unity and alignment because everyone's declarations are shared and supported; you're part of your teammates' practices to improve themselves *for the sake of* their leadership development and the team's success; you see where you can be an offer of help to them; and you're engaged in a team practice. These are all elements that bring people together as a team. In addition, the word *rondori* becomes an operational distinction for a team and how they coordinate together. For example, at the office you ask a team member how they're doing and he or she replies, "I'm in a rondori this morning." It clues you in to what he's facing, and you can ask him if you can help in any way, or, if you had a request for him, you might hold off until a later time or adjust your mood to take into consideration what he's facing.

These are just a few of the practices that one does in the Leadership Dojo. Keep in mind that all the practices and exercises are done against the background of the commitment(s) that one is engaged in and in an environment where the importance of a Leadership Presence quickly becomes visible. The Leadership Dojo is a place where you can safely and rigorously practice, with others and a teacher, those things that will help you fulfill on the future you seek. Some organizations have a "dojo" on site where individuals and teams practice on a daily basis.

Done with recurrence, these types of practices help us see how we fall out of center and allow us to practice recentering. Centering then becomes embodied and our declaration becomes part of who we are.

In our personal or professional lives, we don't put our hands on someone's chest and ask them what they care about. Yet the way we look at someone, our tone of voice, our gestures, requests, feedback, affect her body in the same way as a hand coming toward her. My claim is that by literally touching someone, we learn directly what is too much and what is too little in regard to influencing that person. So when we're in a conversational space, we're able to more clearly sense another's intention, attention, motivation, balance, reactivity, or centeredness after training our nervous system through touch, as described in these practices. At the same time we learn our automatic reactions when under pressure or transition and realize that it's the same if we're physically being touched or if we're "touched" in a conversation with someone.

Practices

- First center and then speak your commitment. What do you notice in your sensation, mood, and thinking?

- Ask a partner/coach/colleague/friend/customer/committed listener to give you feedback when you speak your commitment. What do you notice when you receive the feedback? What shifts in your mood, sensations, and thinking? Is it useful? Are you open to it? Can you incorporate it into your learning?

- Ask your partner to apply a gentle but firm pressure on your chest as you speak your commitment. What do you notice? What do they notice? What do you need to do to more fully embody your commitment?

- Have a partner or partners form a gate with their hands as described earlier. Tell them what the "gate" represents. That is, what obstacle does it represent to fulfilling your commitment? Center, speak your commitment, and then walk through their hands. What is their feedback? What did you notice? Incorporate the feedback and then do it again. What shifts in your sensations, mood, and thinking?

Daily Personal Practices

If we remember that it takes 3,000 repetitions to embody a new skill or behavior, it makes sense to commit to a daily practice outside the dojo in order to build a Leadership Presence. With this in mind, Sylvia committed to two daily practices that would help her stay connected to her declaration of listening. Sylvia chose a sitting practice and a *jo* practice.

During the Leadership Dojo, we introduce participants to four different practices that they can choose to take into their daily lives: sitting, walking, jo practice, or a movement practice. All of these practices are simple and straightforward. The sitting and walking practices require no learning whatsoever since we already know how to sit and walk. The movement and jo practices require learning a set pattern of movements that is called a *kata* in the Japanese martial arts tradition.

In all of these practices there are three ontological elements that produce value. By *ontological* I mean that when this principle is embodied it will be relevant in any endeavor or situation you choose; it will be available wherever you are. It's self-generating and applicable in every circumstance. These three elements go hand in hand with each other and they're indispensable for building a Leadership Presence.

The three ontological elements are:

1 A trained attention,

2 A centered presence, and

3 An embodied commitment.

This means that whatever practice you choose, you will always be developing your attention, your Leadership Presence, and a muscular commitment to action.

In the four practices of sitting, moving, walking, or the jo, we're asked to bring the attention to the life of the body. This does two things: it develops the power of attention, which is central for personal fulfillment and professional success (the element of trained attention); and it builds our Leadership Presence, which is our capacity to be present, open, and grounded (the element of centered presence).

Research, and our common sense, tell us that the ability to concentrate, to be aware of others and our surroundings, to be able to focus attention on a specific point or to open it into a wide periphery, to direct it either inward or outward is essential for fulfillment and success. Recent breakthroughs in neurological research explain how attention plays a critical role in individual and organizational transformation. Neuroscience, with evolved imaging technologies such as functional magnetic resonance imaging (fMRI) and positron emission tomography (PET), along with brain wave analysis, clearly indicates that any behavioral or skill set change is primarily a function of one's ability to focus one's attention on specific distinctions, closely enough, often enough, over an extended period of time. The attention, in plain terms, can be developed like a physical muscle, and these four practices develop the attention and make it stronger, an indispensable skill for a leader. When we have control over our attention, we have more choice, and choice increases our options and our power.

What we pay attention to in these practices is our body; this means sensation, movement, or shape. So while we're developing the muscle of attention we're also developing an expanded somatic awareness, which means an expanded awareness of the self, which increases our Leadership Presence, which increases our capacity to be in action skillfully, compassionately, and wisely.

The third element, the embodiment of our values and commitments, is engaged when you speak your commitment before the beginning of each practice and after the practice is completed.

That is, if you recall the purpose you've engaged in any given activity or practice, it will keep you connected to the commitment of your highest vision. When we're engaged in a practice to help fulfill on our goals, it's critical to remember to stay connected to why we're doing the practice; otherwise it's only a mindless activity. This remembering is an intention that adds scope and depth to the practice that accelerates learning and the ability to manifest our vision.

The importance of remembering why we're practicing was brought home to me in the early '70s when I was with my spiritual teacher in India. After a day of sitting for nearly eight hours straight without moving, I proudly and excitedly told him how long I had sat in meditation. He looked at me intently for a moment and then casually remarked, "A chicken can sit that long." In that moment, and for years following, that single phrase rolled through me with the message of "Pay attention to what you're doing and why you're doing it." Being mindful of the intention and purpose of the activity or practice adds energy and momentum to it.

During her study at the Leadership Dojo, Sylvia learned a *jo kata* (a movement sequence done with a staff *[jo]*, adapted from aikido) and the basic techniques of a sitting meditation practice. Neither of these practices, nor any from the Leadership Dojo, is based in any religious or dogmatic traditions. As mentioned before, Sylvia chose these practices to develop a Leadership Presence and to build a self that could fulfill on her declaration of becoming a more effective listener in her new executive role.

The jo practice helped her see how she pushed forward when she was trying too hard and how this imbalanced her. In the moves in which she extended the jo out, as in a strike, she saw the need to have a strong ground and center so she wouldn't be pulled off her ground. She remarked that this was readily translatable to her professional life when she was thrown off center by her impatience and then ignored people in her headlong effort to complete her list of "things to do."

As Sylvia perfected the thirty-one moves of the jo kata, she began to think of her body as an antenna—a subtle but lively instrument that could receive and transmit nuanced messages from her surroundings. She claimed that in conversations this metaphor of an antenna allowed her to enter into a state of listening that made her a better leader. This translation of the jo practice to her personal and professional life wasn't simply a cognitive insight but a literal change in the way that she related to others. The combined power of embodied practices and one's own energetic narrative transforms into new ways of being, not just information or a new insight.

In the sitting practice Sylvia learned to focus her attention on the sensation of the rising and falling of her abdomen with each breath. When she was distracted by thoughts, sounds, sensations, or anything else, she practiced returning her attention to her breath at the abdomen. Deceptively simple, this practice revealed to Sylvia the constant chatter and restlessness of her mind. She said, "I really never saw how busy and overactive my mind was until I began this practice. Though it was initially painful to see how easily distracted I became, the awareness of my wandering attention was what made it possible for me to return to center and be present."

Very soon this practice transferred into her relationships and made her more present in conversations. "I can now quiet myself by anchoring my attention on my breath, and this allows me to listen more deeply. I can more easily read the moods and attitude of others as well as read between the lines." Her direct reports commented that she seemed more interested in them, and she now had a way of asking questions that told them that there was a new depth to her listening. This increased their trust in her.

Sylvia took her jo to work and set it in the corner by her door. She says that when she looks at it, the jo reminds her of her goals and gives her a sense of added confidence. "I know we weren't learning a martial art, but as a woman, especially a woman who had no sports or martial arts background, it gave me a great sense of empowerment to be able to handle the jo. It's difficult to explain, but learning the thirty-one moves and doing jo practices with my team gave me a sense of mastery that I've never felt before. Sure, I'm successful in my field; it's just different doing it with my body. And it's clear to me that it's positively affected my work life and how I am at home as well."

Practices

- Commit to a daily practice for a minimum of fifteen minutes a day. (Longer, of course, if it works for you, and it's even more effective to have an a.m. and p.m. session. If we pick a length of time that's too long, it's not uncommon for people to become discouraged. In the beginning, pick a time that's manageable, and then increase the time when you're ready.)

- Choose a simple statement that reflects the "for the sake of what" you're engaging in this practice and say it at the beginning and at the end of the practice. For example: "I'm sitting in order to build a centered presence for the sake of writing a book on the Leadership Dojo."

Practices in the Workplace and at Home

To learn new skills and behaviors, it's vital that you practice in the environment in which you want these new skills to appear. This simply means that you practice what it is that you are choosing to transform or create in the environment in which you want it to show up. As an example, Sylvia committed to being in the practice of listening whenever she entered into a conversation with some-one, either in person, on the phone, or by e-mail. This put her prac-tice in real time, directly with the people that she needed to listen to. She would center, remember why it's important to develop this skill, and then be as adept a listener as possible. Sometimes she wouldn't remember, sometimes she would revert to her old behav-iors, but often she found herself fully engaged, and in doing so, felt more personal fulfillment and professional satisfaction. Practices at work, then, are simply practicing what it is that you're cultivating in yourself.

In addition, Sylvia took on an additional practice of centering every time she passed through a doorway in her building. She used this as a way of reminding herself to be aware of her mood, physical comportment, and what she needed to focus on. In an impercep-tible manner, she would take a deep breath, relax, and straighten along her vertical line every time she entered or exited a room. This simple practice was a way for Sylvia to check in with herself throughout the day so she could stay focused and on track.

Practices

- How can you practice in the place that you want to develop a new skill or behavior?

- Write down what it is you are practicing and how you will do it in real time.

- Write down how you can remember to engage in this practice while in work and life.

- Keep a daily log of how you're doing in this practice. Are you successful? Is the new skill or behavior developing? How do you know?

- What shifts in mood do you experience when you take on this practice at work?

WE ARE OUR PRACTICES

The following story reveals another pertinent reason why leaders need to pay attention to what they are practicing. During the late 1990s a strange set of circumstances appeared around the shooting of an Arizona highway patrolman in a remote part of the Southwest desert. Reconstructing the events around his death, it became clear that the patrolman had stopped someone, they had a shootout, he had wounded his assailant, but the shooter was able to drive off after killing the officer. What was odd in this tragic story was that the dead highway patrolman's weapon was holstered and the six spent shells of the rounds he had fired were found in the front left breast pocket of his uniform. It confounded the investigators until it was revealed that the training procedure at the firing range for this highway patrolman's section was to fire off six rounds, pick up the casings, and then put them in the left front breast pocket. He simply did what he had been practicing, even when it was a live, dangerous event.

The story of the highway patrolman is a dramatic illustration, however grim, that we are what we practice. As incredulous as it may seem, this incident points to the hard truth that, under pressure, 99.9 percent of us will precipitate to our level of practice. When we're under pressure, stress, conflict, or some form of transition, we will inevitably fall to the level of our training and rarely, if ever, rise to our level of expectation. It's critical for leaders to choose their practices wisely and to engage in them with conscious intent. The value and necessity of practice in sports, recreational activities, or the performing arts is part of our common sense. But it utterly escapes us when we think of practices for leadership and building character virtues within business, the military, government, public institutions, or at home.

The claim of the Leadership Dojo is that leadership is a skill and art that can be trained through recurrent practices, just as one learns how to swing a golf club, ski, or hit a tennis ball. It's possible to strengthen a muscle such as a bicep; it is equally possible to train the muscles of integrity, confidence, collaboration, courage, and empathy. We can build muscles in every dimension of our lives, including the physical, emotional, mental, and spiritual. The catch is to practice and to go beyond our comfort zones.

At an even more fundamental level it's necessary to come to terms with the fact that we are *always* practicing. In other words, the body is incapable of not practicing. And what we practice we become. Our biology is organized to take in stimulus from the environment, and we then shape ourselves to cope with and effectively deal with that stimulus. Even as you sit here reading this book, you are shaping yourself by your posture, the way you're breathing, what you're thinking, feeling, and sensing. While this may seem subtle and far below the level of our awareness, over time this has a powerful effect in how we are shaped, and this shape affects how we perceive the world and conversely how the world perceives us.

For example, the next time you're walking down the street, notice the expressions on people's faces and the way they hold their bodies. Notice the down-turned mouths, the hunched shoulders, the scowls, grimaces, and then the rare few whose faces reflect joy and a positive attitude toward life, and imagine for yourself what they've been practicing. The way we comport ourselves is a direct reflection of what we've been practicing.

Because it does not live in our common sense that we change through practices, we live in hope and fantasy about people and cultures changing by simply being introduced to a new idea. The consequences of this can be a downward spiral of frustration, resignation, and ultimately despair. Take the recent example of the so-called liberation of Iraq. George Packer, a correspondent living in Baghdad, wrote in the *New Yorker* that "Iraqis were told they were free, they expected to be free, they had been waiting for years to be free—but they still didn't feel free. And so a depression set in almost at once." In the same article, Akila al-Hashemi, one of the three women appointed to the governing council and who was fifteen when the Baath Party took power, was quoted as saying, "We are still under the shock, we are still afraid. Now I'm fifty. You see? You can imagine—can I change in two days, in two months, in two years?"

Packer further quotes from a prospectus of the Gilgamesh Center for Creative Thinking written by Dr. Baher Buti, an Iraqi psychiatrist, who states that the Iraqi people "lack the power to experience freedom, they don't comprehend the correct performance of democracy, they cannot deal with group working...."[3] After thirty-five years of living under the iron fist of the Baath Party, the Iraqis' expectation—and that of invaders and occupiers—was that the Iraqis would suddenly become model citizens engaged in an active, thriving democracy. When this didn't occur—as it didn't when Poland turned to democracy after decades of communism— a mood of resentment and then despondency took over.

When the traditional paradigm of learning is teachers talk, students listen, and knowledge is in books, it should be no surprise that our expectations fall short when we are asked to take on new roles without the proper practices. Books, DVDs, or a one-day seminar cannot teach leadership. It's necessary, nay critical, that emerging leaders commit to practices that allow them to embody new ways of being and acting.

THE RANGE OF EMBODIED BEHAVIORS

Embodied behaviors include reflexes, habits, routines, practices, and generative practices.

A *reflex* is an involuntary physiological response as a result of the nervous system's reaction to a stimulus. This could be a sneeze, which is triggered by a nerve impulse sent from a nerve center in response to a nerve receptor's reaction to a stimulus. Another example is the gag reflex. If something is lodged in our throat or if our throat is touched too firmly we will cough or gag reflexively. A reflex is hardwired in our nervous system. Reflexes are factory-loaded; they come with having a body. There is no choice, training, or practice required for the reflex to be engaged.

A habit and a routine are the outcomes of training in certain practices. A *habit* is a behavior that is regular, repetitive, and un-conscious. In the West, for example, when two people meet for the first time they have the habit of shaking hands. In the same situation in India, they will place their hands together and bow to each other. As a social habit, this is an unconsidered behavior in the sense that it does not have to be at the level of conscious thought to be enacted. When it's learned at an early age, there is choice and it is done consciously. But the behavior quickly recedes to the background of our consciousness, and we simply find ourselves ex-tending our hand when we meet someone. We're not exercising conscious choice. In our inquiry of training leaders, we do not use the term *habit* to describe a behavior that is embodied, although that's what it is. We don't use *habit* because it connotes uncon-sciousness and something that may be "negative," as in a "bad" habit like smoking, or it's trivialized as "only" a habit.

A *routine* is the way a set of tasks is arranged that is typically repetitive and unvarying. Routines may have longer horizons of time, like one's routine for a week. Or a routine may have a shorter horizon of time, as in your routine after you come home from work. Routines are also embodied, but again they connote an unreflec-tive behavior that lacks the element of choice. Like habits, routines are often inherited or unconsciously adopted from our family of origin, culture, media influences, or the social groups with which we spend most of our time. They are often not behaviors that we consciously commit to as part of our lives. We find ourselves in a particular drift, and in this lack of conscious intent we embody habits and routines that are present in our behaviors but remain in the background of our awareness. Habits may be useful, like how we drive our cars, or harmful, like smoking, but in either case they become so much a part of us we do not live with them as if we're making a choice.

A *practice* is a conscious choice we make to train ourselves so we will behave and act in a particular way so that it becomes embodied or part of who we are. To choose a practice is to have a narrative why one is committing to this practice. For example, one may choose not to eat anything or drink alcohol three hours before going to bed because we know we will sleep more soundly or that it will help us lose weight. One may choose a practice of saving money every month as a way to prepare for a child's college education.

A *generative practice* is a conscious choice to embody a behavior that can be used in whatever situation we find ourselves. It's a commitment to a way of being in the world. It is life-affirming, creative, and it produces a reality by how we orient to our life situation. Learning to type, on the other hand, is a specific practice; it's specific to a certain context and it takes care of a specific concern. But typing is useful only when we're typing. A generative practice we can use anytime, anyplace, even when we're learning to type. Generative practices are what we focus on in the Leadership Dojo in producing exemplary leaders. In this case, we are the practice.

Practices

- Make a list of the habits and routines you're currently engaged in. Are these habits and routines relevant to who you're becoming as a leader and where you want to go? If so, write why, and if not, why not?

- Write down what new practices would assist you in becoming who you want to be and where you want to go.

- What would be a generative practice that would increase your ability to be an exemplary leader?

- Make a commitment to a generative practice. Commit to a certain period of time and keep a journal about your learning.

In Chapters Five and Six we look at the core practices in the Leadership Dojo and how they form the base for building exemplary leaders.

FIVE

The Body of a Leader

But the awakened and knowing say: body am
I entirely, and nothing else; and soul is only a
word for something about the body. Behind your
thoughts and feelings, my brother, there stands a
mighty ruler, an unknown sage—whose name is
self. In your body he dwells; he is your body.

Friedrich Nietzsche, *Thus Spake Zarathustra*

■ ■ ■

I n the beginning is the body. We are born into a body, and
through the body we come to know the world and ourselves.
Other bodies orbit about and we join them in the dance of coming together and moving apart. Gestures and sounds emanate from
the body into language and thinking. With language incarnate we
live consciously in time and rhythmically with others. Our embodied life extends into a horizon of possibility in which the past is
history in our flesh, the present is the center of being and action,

and the future is the trajectory of our felt imagination. It is only as a body that we are present and make sense to others. Our bodily presence is the unmistakable way that we become evident to others, the environment, and the world. This is so obvious that it's invisible to us.

Consider this: Without the body there is nothing to reflect upon, to touch, to feel, to think about, to enter into relationship with. Without the body the possibility of contact with others or oneself is simply not possible. It is only through our bodies—our ability to see, hear, touch, sense, taste, feel, gesture, intuit, speak, and think—that we are able to be in relationship with other bodies, other presences, the world. It's the body that allows us to navigate through the layered shadows of grief and the complexity of happiness; it's the body that tells us whether we trust others ... or not; it is in our bodies that we risk ourselves and learn from our mistakes; it is through the body that we discover significance and know what we care about; it is the body that generates mood and interacts effectively with others.

The body is not only central to our capacity to fully live our lives and to lead others; it's inseparable from the self. The idea of a self, or mind, that is independent of the body is an error of rationalistic thinking. The physical body is a reflection of who we are. The European philosopher Ludwig Wittgenstein remarked that if you want an image of the soul, look at the human body. Or consider the assembly of terms that are part of our everyday speech that draw the self and body together and are at once moral and physical when we characterize others: *tender, prickly, callous, heavy, stiff, cold-blooded, warm-hearted, heartless, bruised, sensitive, sharp, rough,*

86

thick- or thin-skinned, hot-blooded, scared out of my body, spine-less, someone being under my skin, and so on.

Layered deep within our tissues, our cells, in our DNA, beneath the concepts of body as anatomy and machine, lives a wisdom out of which our reality is directly formed. This animating power informs our being-ness in the world. The energy of this living body, which the phenomenological philosopher Maurice Merleau-Ponty called the "body subject," is the very power that emboldened my fingers in a flurry of movement to type these words. It's the intelligence that allows me to feel that the car is going too fast around a slippery curve without looking at the speedometer, to notice that the mood of a teammate is off without him saying anything, to soften under the gaze of a baby, to wince when a loved one is in pain, to lift up in glee, to take up space with dignity, to stiffen when a stranger enters uninvited into my space.

But it is not me, the "I" we are so fond of, who commands these actions like the chairman of the board, for in my depths I *am* these sensations, as my gratefulness is indistinguishable from a warmth in my chest, or my wariness is intimately linked with a metallic sensation galvanized on the edge of my skin, or my joy can only be artificially separated from the breath that is a wave through my rib-cage. When we live from the wisdom and intelligence of the lived body, our gestures, sensations, and utterances bring to life feelings, images, moods, actions, and yearnings without the intermediary of thought. Taking action from this ground of *being* is the foundation of exemplary leadership.

But we've been taught to keep our body at a distance, as if it were an indiscreet waiter to be kept in the background until needed. We call upon it to deliver us to our intellectual appointments and to be appropriate while doing so. We are taught to attend to the body only when something goes wrong, as we do with computer hard drives and air conditioners, and because we think of the body as a complex machine we deliver its broken parts or rusty systems to medical technologies "to be repaired." Or we identify the body with the unblemished, airbrushed figures we see on magazine covers, with the religious dogma that tells us that the flesh is the ticket to hell, or with a curious narcissism in which the body is pampered and patronized as something apart, like a museum piece.

Marginalizing the body, even despising it, has a long history in philosophy and science, beginning with Socrates, shaped by Galileo, refined by Descartes, and institutionalized by the church and schools. Our educational system reflects this tradition of separating mind and body, spirit and matter, emotions and self, and the list goes on, by virtually eliminating a curriculum that places the body as the locus of experience. Robert M. Hutchins, a founder of the University of Chicago, is famous for saying, "Whenever I feel like exercise, I lie down until the feeling passes." In the twenty-first century a growing cadre of Internet enthusiasts carry on this lineage of denying the body when they assert that cyberspace will allow us to transcend the limits of our body. John Perry Barlow, one of the leading figures in this electronic frontier, says the Net will be "a world that is both everywhere and nowhere, but it is not where bodies live."[1]

The momentum to drive the body into irrelevance has severely limited our potential for creating wise leaders. It's important to understand that it is only through our bodies that we are able to be unwaveringly present to people and situations, a necessary requirement for exemplary leadership all but categorically denied by modern philosophy. If we think of the body as only a footnote to our lives we cannot fully grasp who we are, what we are, the kind of world we live in, and why we yearn for what we yearn for. This is the self-knowledge that separates intelligent technicians from exemplary leaders.

The body in the Leadership Dojo is radically different from the body that we have been taught to anatomize, idealize, or loathe. The body I speak of expresses our history, commitments, dignity, wounds, authenticity, identity, roles, moral strength, moods, emotional resilience, and aspirations as a unique quality of aliveness we call the "self." In this interpretation, the body and the self are indistinguishable. The body is where thought begins, since the body is where we are. We view the world in the way that we do because of the bodies that we are. That is, the way we organize ourselves opens and closes our possibilities in the world.

The body we are will be the type of leader we are.

For example, think of the person whose shoulders are rounded, her head pitched forward, her chest sunken. This contraction and shortening in the chest and shoulder girdle places pressure on the internal organs—the heart, lungs, esophagus, and stomach crowd against each other. In this reduced space the capacity of these organs to correspond with each other and the rest of the body is significantly reduced. The system is compromised, and the resulting stress reduces effective action, emotional balance, physical health, and mental alertness. In this position, oxygen and blood transportation is diminished to the limbs as well as to the other organs, including the brain, and one's thinking becomes dull, lacking sharpness.

Because the head is thrust forward and the spine rounded in compensation one is constantly struggling against gravity to maintain balance and equilibrium. The long muscles along the spine and neck ache from the chronic effort to be upright. This dull, nagging pain dogs the attention and makes it difficult to stay present with others and to concentrate on the business at hand.

We can see that this way of holding ourselves taxes our capacity to have a positive, can-do attitude. We cannot breathe deeply enough; there is insufficient blood flowing to our vital organs; we are in low-grade chronic pain; and because of the way we're slouched downward with our hunching shoulders and drooping head, our view of the world is limited. Our neural, sensory, and muscular organization—the way we think, feel, and act—presents us with a specific environment about which to think, feel, and act. In other words, the person I described earlier would consider the world differently if she were upright, relaxed, and in harmony with gravity, instead of caved in and relinquishing power. Just as a salamander cannot consider nature the same way Wordsworth could, not only because it cannot read "Intimations on Immortality," but because its body allows it only to take in a square inch at a time. If we are dominated by a contracted or otherwise imbalanced body, and because of its volume of sensation (read: pain and discomfort), we will be unable to think clearly, be empathetic, or create trust with others.

My example is by no means an exaggeration. Every day, for the past thirty-six years, I have seen individuals, entrepreneurs, corporate executives, government policy makers, pastors, and military leaders who have abdicated their bodies and in doing so have severely limited the depth and scope of their potential.

Now consider the perspective others have toward the individual I described earlier. We ask ourselves, as we always do, when we stand in front of someone: If this is my leader, can I trust him? Will she fulfill on her promises? Can he take effective action toward his goals? Is she reliable? Will I enjoy working with him? Will she create a positive, generous mood? Can she create a unified team? With a body that is caved in, as in our example, it's difficult for others to be mobilized and motivated by this individual, even though she is a decent, competent, well-meaning person. In other words, the way that one organizes oneself bodily will produce assessments from others that will open and close possibilities.

The way we shape ourselves will have people move toward us, away from us, against us, or be indifferent to us.

When I am hunched and coiling inward, I am predisposed to resignation; neck and shoulders rigid, chest unyielding make it difficult for me to empathize with others; squinting at others sideways makes them suspicious of me. Actions reflect the self. The self is not what we think or say about ourselves, but how we act, and how others perceive us. There's an illuminating story about Abraham Lincoln that speaks depths about this marriage of body and self.

Lincoln was interviewing a candidate for a position in his administration. He had an assistant with him during the interview process and when it was finished the assistant asked him if he had made a decision. When Lincoln replied that he would not nominate the candidate, the assistant asked him why.

"I don't like his face," Lincoln replied.

"How can you disqualify someone because of their face?" the assistant asked incredulously. "It's just their face."

"After forty everyone's responsible for their face," Lincoln replied.

Lincoln was pointing directly to the connection between the shape we are, our body, and who we are. History now shows that Lincoln had an uncanny way of reading others.[2]

Consider the skill of creating trust, an essential leadership quality for motivating others. We may read a book on trust and understand it intellectually, but if we do not embody this understanding we will not produce trust in others. That is, if our body (the self) is not organized to observe mood (trust), or is not structured in a way that will allow others to assess us as trustworthy, this skill of observing mood and building trust will be unavailable to us. Inside our own thinking we may be sincere, acknowledging the importance of trust as valuable for our work. But if our breath is high and rapid in our chest, if we're squeezing our eyes, and if there's a frozen smile on our faces, we will ourselves have difficulty trusting, and it will be difficult for others to trust us. There is a very real difference between talking about trust and being trust.

The bodies that we are will be the leaders that we will be.

The body is the shape of our experience. This shape affects the world and the world affects our shape. This shape is our lived, felt experience that produces both a worldview and an identity in the world. There are practices we can engage in that will change our shape and thus change our worldview, which in turn makes us more effective as leaders and human beings. This is a radical departure from the centuries-old notion in Western culture that the rational mind can untangle all of our tough problems. This is not to degrade the value of our intellectual faculties, but we need to recognize that we've become imbalanced and it's critical that we right the balance toward the wisdom of the life of the body.

SOMATICS: THE UNITY OF MIND/BODY/SPIRIT

In the Leadership Dojo, we claim that the body can be shaped to create a Leadership Presence of skillful action, grounded compassion, and pragmatic wisdom.

This idea of the bodily life being the locus of leadership and mastery is based in the philosophical and psychological discourse called "somatics." Somatics is from the Greek word *soma*, which literally translates as "the living body in its wholeness."[3] Wholeness in this sense includes the physical world of sensations, temperature, weight, movement, streaming, pulsation, and vibrations, as well as our images, thoughts, stories, attitudes, yearnings, dreams, and language. The somatic notion of wholeness pre-dates the Cartesian mind/body separation. This is the early Greek ideal in which athletic prowess, mental clarity, emotional balance, and a moral and ethical vision were seen as the requirements for the burgeoning citizenry of the new nation-states. From this point of view, every person is a soma; in our present vernacular it's often referred to as the mind/body/spirit unity.

Somatics declares the human form as the space in which humans act, relate, think, feel, and express emotions and moods. In this interpretation, the body is the field in which we build trust and intimacy, produce meaningful work, create family, community, and teams, bring forth a world in language, and live our spiritual longing. In this view human beings are recognized as a unity that expresses biological, linguistic, historical, social, and spiritual lives. This is radically different from traditional thinking, which separates mind, body, and spirit. To work somatically in creating leadership is to work with the unity of the human organism. To do this, we first observe how life takes shape in the individual and how the individual shapes him- or herself toward life. We then create a set of practices that allows a new shape to emerge, to come to life.

One of the most remarkable discoveries of modern neuroscience is that the body controls the brain (read: mind) as much as the mind controls the body. While ancient traditions such as yoga, martial arts, Oriental medicine, and meditation have shown this for centuries, it's grounding and comforting to have science assure us that this is so from an empirical point of view. The work of Paul Eckman, Ph.D., a professor of psychology and director of the Human Interaction Laboratory at the University of California Medical School in San Francisco, has graphically shown how deeply the body affects mind and emotions. Since the 1960s Eckman has been studying facial expressions in regard to emotions. Recently he's built an international reputation in the field of interrogation and lie detection based on his work of reading micro-expressions in the face.

At one point when he and a colleague were researching emotional expressions by forming their facial muscles into the shape of a specific emotion, Eckman stumbled upon a startling truth about mind and body. At the end of a day of emulating and practicing the muscular shape of sadness, he realized that he felt very, very sad. His colleague corroborated this, and they then began to track their reactions as they spent hours shaping the muscles of their faces into a particular emotion. "We weren't expecting this at all. And it happened to both of us. We felt *terrible*. What we were generating was sadness, anguish."

He experienced the same things with other emotions; his heartbeat increased ten to twelve beats when he shaped his face into the expression of anger, and his hands significantly heated up.

> What we discovered is that expression alone is sufficient to create marked changes in the autonomic nervous system. If you intentionally make a facial expression, you change your physiology. By making the correct expression, you begin to have the changes in your physiology that accompany the emotion. The face is not simply a means of display, but also a means of activating emotion. In other words, simply putting the face into a smile drives the brain to activity typical of happiness—just as a frown does with sadness.[4]

This also means that an expression you do not know you have can create an emotion you're not consciously choosing. By becoming more aware of our bodies, we have more choice over the emotions and moods that we experience.

Somatics is a pragmatic philosophy grounded in a set of practices. These practices produce a Leadership Presence in which you learn to be present to others while staying firmly grounded in what you care about: the capacity to generate trust and repair it when it's broken, to have empathy and respect for others, to listen deeply, to act with authenticity and purpose, to coordinate effectively with others, and to be a lifelong learner. Training the body in this sense doesn't mean losing weight, building big biceps, having a flat stomach, or hitting a golf ball a long way; it means training the spirit for leadership. It's the commitment to building powerful, wise, and compassionate leaders who have the capacity to be self-generating, self-healing, and self-educating.

It is the somatic element, the grounding in physical practices, that allows these principles to become embodied as new skills and behaviors instead of being limited to a theoretical reality without practical application. In the Leadership Dojo, people learn to be leaders by taking new actions from a centered presence, not by simply acquiring new information. Somatic practices allow us to embody leadership virtues and principles; this step toward action and change in behavior is not accessible by cognitive understanding alone.

A NEW INTERPRETATION OF THE BODY

Working with somatic practices to build leaders requires a new interpretation of what we mean by *body*. The "Body of a Leader" consists of five domains:

1 Action

2 Mood

3 Coordination

4 Learning

5 Dignity

As we look at these five domains, it's important to remember that we separate them only as a convenience for understanding them because in reality they comprise a whole. They compose one thing, the bodyself, and it's only a conceit of language that we separate them. It's these five domains that we train in the Leadership Dojo.

Action

> I have always thought the actions of men
> the best interpreters for their thoughts.
>
> John Locke

The word *leadership* derives from the Old English *Lethin,* which means "to make happen, to make go." Leaders take action. Action is based in our muscular system. Leaders create a vision and then mobilize and organize others (or themselves) toward an observable goal. We can see the results of their actions. But action is not necessarily movement. Action is connected with a powerful story of care. In other words, if our actions are not directly connected to a narrative of what matters to us, and why it matters, we are simply performing tasks, going about our days tediously completing a checklist. We get things done when we perform tasks, but with our nose to the grindstone we're disconnected from the bigger picture. When we're connected to why we're doing something through a narrative that tells us "for the sake of what" we're taking the action, we're more effective, our mood is more generative, we're focused, and we operate in a larger horizon of time. We are most deeply connected to our "for the sake of what" when we've thought through what it is that matters to us; this is a narrative of care. Take, for example, the single mother of three who holds down three jobs. Because she knows that she's committed to having her children go to college, she finds meaning and purpose in what she's doing and she can live in a mood of fulfillment instead of resentment.

Leaders, then, put their narrative of care into a declaration, which is a commitment to a future.[5] For example: "I will grow the business 15 percent this year." "We will reinvigorate our Social Security system." "Every family in America will have adequate health care." "Our military will be equipped with the most advanced technology available." "I will lose twenty-five pounds in the next six months." "I will write a book." "I will lead the PTA to a 20 percent increase in enrollment by the beginning of the year." Behind each of these commitments is a story (we commonly think of it as an explanation) of why it is important.

This points to a critical piece of somatics and leadership: language is a bodily phenomena and not the result of a disembodied mind. Our thinking and stories arise from our body, our nervous system, and are directly related to how and why we act. Our stories are not just breath going through our vocal chords to form words. When a person embodies his or her story we say, "He *is* the commitment; she *is* the story." The commitment is not apart from the person but is embodied in his or her thoughts, words, and actions. Think of Martin Luther King Jr.'s "I Have a Dream" speech. He wasn't simply making a speech about a good idea; he *was* the story. He embodied this possibility for the future. This means that in training exemplary leadership it's necessary to develop practices in which leaders become the story of the future, and they're not simply reciting a speech. When this occurs the individual is seen as authentic, committed, and coherent. Our trust for them has grown and we want to move forward with them.

The following parable of the stonecutters is a useful metaphor in understanding the connection between language, story, and action. Imagine three stonecutters, each with a mallet in one hand and a cold chisel in the other, sitting on a stool in front of a huge block of granite. To the casual observer it looks as if they are all doing the same thing, cutting on a slab of stone. They are, in other words, all engaged in the same activity.

When we ask the first stonecutter what he's doing, he replies, "I'm carving a piece of stone."

We move to the second stonecutter and ask her what she's doing. "I'm building a wall," she says.

When we ask the same question of the third stonecutter, he answers, "I'm creating a cathedral."

The activity is cutting the stone. We're always involved in some activity, such as running meetings, engaging in conversations, reading e-mails, assessing performance, making requests, planning the future, balancing the budget, and so forth. The first stonecutter is simply engaged in the task of the activity. His only story is that he's cutting a piece of stone. There's minimal or no connection to why he's doing his task and therefore no passion in it. This is the person who attends the meeting because he was told to, and he positions himself as a victim, or a detached observer at best, acting as if he has no choice or accountability in the matter. "I was told to be here so here I am" is the refrain. This puts the individual in a mood of resentment about being there. He lacks commitment and a larger vision of contribution. This is not leadership.

The second stonecutter has a bigger picture. She has a story that her activity is connected to something more than just chipping away on a stone. She's constructing a wall that will be part of a future building. But her story ends at the wall. Perhaps she's a wall expert or wall technician, but her sense of purpose and meaning goes no further. This is the person who is committed to being present at the meeting and participates in the discussion, but does not own the outcome or results.

The third stonecutter lives in the biggest story. As he's engaged in the activity of cutting the stone, he consistently holds the narrative of the cathedral. He may recognize that his vision of a cathedral may not be achieved in his lifetime or even that of his children, but his commitment and focus play a significant role in its completion. Think what it would be like if throughout your day and the various activities you're engaged in you remember the "cathedral" you're building. This is the person who "owns" the meeting. She's in full ownership and accountable to how the meeting turns out. She takes full agency over the activities she's chosen and is committed to the mood, actions, thinking, and direction of the conversation. This produces a positive mood, focus, accountability, creative thinking, and a deep listening to what is needed.

We say that it is the third stonecutter who is most in action. When we're connected to our activities by a story, by a vision of what is important that drives our intention, we say we're "in action." If we move about our day mindlessly from one task to another, we're not in action. In order to take skillful action as a leader one must embody an idea (or vision) and values. The Sufis have a saying that reflects this notion: *Dast ba Dar, Del ba Yar* ("While your hands are in your work, keep your Heart with God"). In the Leadership Dojo, leaders are taught how to act skillfully while embodying their "cathedral" stories. They embody the story, so they *are* the story. What they say, how they are, and what they do are congruent. This builds trust and mobilizes people to collaborate and take action with the leader.

Mood

> If you want to lead, know what you're doing with your energy.
>
> Lao Tzu

Peter Drucker, America's management and leadership guru for the past forty years, has said that the primary job of a leader is to manage his or her energy. When you think of all the things a leader attends to, this is a remarkable statement. Managing our energy falls into the domain of mood. Mood is our orientation to a given situation. It's our disposition and outlook on life. It's the quality of our energy in a situation. We also call this *esprit, spirit, energy, attitude,* or *feeling,* as in, What's your mood? How's your energy? How's the esprit, or spirit, of the team? Or, How are you feeling? How's their attitude?

Mood is different than emotion in that moods live in a longer horizon of time, while emotions usually exist for a shorter span of time. Moods also have a strong influence on what emotions we experience. For example, if we're in a mood of curiosity and openness, it's difficult to be angry, while a persistent mood of resentment is a breeding ground for anger and even rage. Mood is our being-ness in the world. Think of someone you know well; if asked to describe him you would include his being-ness. For example, we think of others as being upbeat, sour, withdrawn, sunny, positive, peaceful, scattered, resentful, focused, and so forth. Mood is a cornerstone in how we perceive and relate to the world and others. Our mood, or way of being in the world, is like a compass bearing; it sets our course and it opens and closes possibilities.

The way we manage our moods is critical to how others relate to us and to our own success and fulfillment. We can have unlimited resources, be connected to the right people, have a good education, but if our mood is off—if we're resigned, for example—it will be difficult to generate sufficient passion and energy to move a project or enterprise forward, either on our own merits or by motivating others. In aikido we speak about projecting positive *ki* or energy. This means we take every challenge and crisis as an opportunity for transformation and a positive outcome. This is living in a mood of possibility, one of the most powerful moods for leadership and living.

Mood is a bodily phenomenon, not a mental construct in which we put on a happy face and hope or think ourselves into an attitude change. We may be "acting" differently by putting on a different face and assuming new behaviors, but we'll appear and feel inauthentic. By changing our shape—that is, how we organize ourselves bodily—we're able to shift our mood, how we're being in the world. When we change our mood in this way, we can better see the moods of others. It's fundamental for leaders to observe moods and to be able to affect them in a positive way. If leaders are blind to the domain of mood, it's as if they're navigating a ship without a compass.

I worked with a woman who was promoted to an executive leadership role after years of strong performance as an accountant in a large financial services company. She was rational, forward thinking, extremely competent, took great pride in her technical expertise, and accordingly received accolades for it. But when she became head of the finance department in her multinational company, she quickly ran into trouble. Simply said, she didn't notice the people she was leading. This was not only because she spent her days buried in her office with most of her professional interactions conducted by e-mail or phone, but because her team never appeared on her radar as multidimensional humans with moods, emotions, and concerns. She moved competently through all the activities of her new role, but her direct reports quickly began to complain about her as being too busy and not present. Soon the performance of the team plummeted and the team existed in a mood of resignation and began to isolate from her. She was blind to all of this, and when it was pointed out to her she was perplexed. Because she was sincere and wanted to succeed she worked at it, but she did so from a tips-and-techniques perspective and it perplexed her even more that her efforts didn't produce the desired results. Faithful to her discourse as an accountant, she thought if she followed a formula and balanced the ledger—that is, read the right books and got it "right"—she would "understand this mood thing" and her team could get back to work.

The work was, as all this work is, simple yet comprehensive. To shift her pattern it was necessary for her to notice what she felt. This informed her of her moods and the fundamental power of moods, sensitizing her to the moods and emotions of those around her. Once this happened she began to listen to her team in new ways, and this opened the gate to mobilizing them with more speed and care. But the first thing she had to do was to be alive in her own body, to notice how and what moods she created.

To be an exemplary leader it's necessary to take on new practices that will move us out of our heads and into our bodies.

Coordination

> My belief is in the blood and flesh as being wiser than the
> intellect. The body unconscious is where life bubbles up in us. It
> is how we know that we are alive, alive to the depth of our souls
> and in touch somewhere with the vivid reaches of the cosmos.
>
> D. H. Lawrence

In the Leadership Dojo, the foundation for effective coordination
is directly linked to how we live in our bodies. There is, of course,
the necessity for making strategies and plans, having a collective
vision, creating a mission statement, agreeing to a set of values, and
having a table of organization in which there are appointed roles,
tasks, and commitments. But at the end of the day it is *how* we are,
our living presence, that allows effective coordination to take place.
An organization can have elegantly framed mission statements on
the walls of its meeting rooms and there can be well-defined lines
of communication between individuals and departments, but if the
people are not present, open, and connected to others, they will
not be able to coordinate in a way that moves the action forward
with everyone's dignity intact.

One of the major mistakes in this domain is thinking that "being clear" is the essential requirement for effective coordination.
During a breakdown in communication when someone pleads that
"I was clear," "I clearly told them," "I said it numerous times," "It
was obvious what had to be done," or "They said they were clear,"
it normally points out that this "clarity" exists solely in the speaker's mind. In other words, we believe that if we think we're clear
about what has to be done, and if we communicate understandable
words, coordination will naturally follow. If clarity is seen only as

the relaying of information from one head to another, effective co-ordination will not necessarily follow. Coordination is about taking action; it's not about someone repeating verbatim what you said to them. If action is the standard for coordination, then my dog Rosie and I are far more effective at communicating with each other than are many of the "clear"-speaking, educated people I see running organizations.

Clarity is useful in coordinating with others only when it produces an interpretation shared by all concerned, and when all parties act in accordance with that interpretation. In order to do this we must be present to others. In order to be present to others we must be present to ourselves. The surest way to be present to ourselves, and therefore to others, is to live in our bodies, which is to live inside our own experience.

Clearly effective coordination requires making commitments to others in language through requests and promises and other speech acts. However, if we're not paying attention to the bodies of those we're interacting with, what comes out of their mouths may be inconsistent with what they can or cannot do. In other words, a person may say he's committing to something, but when we look at his body we can see that he may not be able to manage the commitment; that is, although he may want to fulfill it, he may not embody the competency to do what he promises.

Or, we may see that someone, despite her sincerity, doesn't have the body to manage the situation if she suddenly finds she's unable to keep the commitment. Instead of reporting the problem, she feels paralyzed by shame, and to avoid embarrassment she doesn't communicate the breakdown, which causes further problems downstream and breaks trust. We can train ourselves to see whether someone has the body, or not, to build and maintain the relationship in an ongoing way to produce trust, satisfaction, and fulfillment.

What I am saying is that from a somatic point of view there's a way of feeling into someone to help determine the best way to coordinate with that person, or not. Coordination in this sense has to do with the unification of speech, action, and mood. We can train ourselves to be in harmony with other bodies for effective coordination, and we can train ourselves to observe bodies so that our ability to accurately assess someone's sincerity, competence, and reliability in fulfilling on commitments is enhanced.

The result of effective coordination is to move the mission forward, respect others, and remain flexible to the changes that will inevitably occur.

Learning

> We need to encourage habits of flexibility, of continuous learning—for institutions as well as for individuals.
>
> Peter Drucker

Learning is a bodily phenomenon, and it occurs through practice and recurrence. If I want to learn a new computer program, for example, it's not enough just to read the instructions. Nor will I gain competency by memorizing the sequence of certain functions. To be able to employ the program without having to consciously deliberate over my moves requires practicing over time. When we think of how we learned to drive a car, we can see the common sense in this. We first distinguished the various parts—gas pedal, brake, steering wheel, turn signals, speedometer, and so on. Then we began to cautiously and self-consciously drive under the tutelage of a teacher. Now we drive and converse with other passengers, plan our day, listen to music, daydream, and even talk on the phone. The ability to drive a car is embodied. It's invisible to us. It's so transparent to us that it may even be difficult to teach to someone else. It's something we just do. Through a practice of recurrent actions, we've embodied the capacity to drive without having to consciously reflect on how we're doing it. We can now say we have the body for driving a car.

In today's world we're continually required to learn new skills. It's not enough to simply be knowledgeable about something; it's necessary to act and perform in new ways. We're not suggesting that we abandon cognitive learning. We are saying that it's only one aspect of learning. We do see, however, that learning happens in our bodies. When we understand, for example, the power of making grounded assessments, requests, and offers, but find ourselves incompetent to do so, it's necessary to design practices that train our bodies to skillfully make these speech acts. Once we're able to perform these actions in a recurrent, graceful manner, we say, "He has the body for making requests"; or, "She has the body of a leader"; or, "He doesn't have the body for making offers." Here we return again to the words of William Shakespeare, "By my actions, teach my mind."

When we take new actions, perform in new ways, or behave differently, we're seen as someone who has learned something new. The converse is true in that if we don't embody new actions and behaviors we'll be assessed as not learning, as not growing and evolving; or, putting it in another way, not keeping up. Take, for example, a manager who is evaluated as not fulfilling on his promises. He decides to learn about keeping commitments to satisfy his customers and his boss. He reads the latest books on commitment and responsibility. He becomes intellectually knowledgeable on the subject and can speak convincingly about it, yet nothing changes in his actions. Despite his knowledge of the subject, he continues to find himself failing his commitments. Regardless of his understanding and theories about commitments, he has not changed his actions and continues to be assessed as someone who has not learned and therefore cannot be trusted. What is missing is a set of practices that will allow him to modify his body in a way that shows consistency with his declaration of keeping his commitments.

Learning through our body opens many possibilities for us. We see that we can grow and transform and we see how we can coach others to grow and learn. Through bodily learning we become more capable of producing a future that takes care of our loved ones and us.

Dignity

> Get up, Stand up,
> Stand up for your right!
> Bob Marley

The drive for dignity is a fundamental characteristic of all human beings. Humans have an innate desire to be recognized as having worth, as being valuable to others, to be held in esteem. We want to matter to others. This creates a proper sense of pride and self-respect, which is the condition of being worthy of respect, esteem, and honor.

Our capacity for choice is the foundation for a life of dignity. As moral agents we have the power to make choices that transcend our small-mindedness and desire for safety. When we choose to be more than a random collection of fears, impulses, and emotions we have taken the first step in claiming our dignity. Choosing a life of dignity produces purpose, meaning, and care. Vaclav Havel, the playwright and former President of Czechoslovakia, spoke about it in this way: "The essential aims of life are present naturally in every person. In everyone there is some longing for humanity's rightful dignity, for moral integrity, for free expression of being, and a sense of transcendence over the world of existences."[6]

At the beginning of the Western philosophical tradition, Plato opens the question of dignity in his *Republic*. In the *Republic*, Socrates, in conversation with two Athenian aristocrats, calls for a class of citizens who can defend their cities from external enemies. He says the chief characteristic of these guardian citizens is *thymos*, a Greek word that roughly translates as a "spiritedness," or "heartedness." He goes on to explain that thymos is associated with courage, indignation, self-esteem, and the capacity to fight for what is right and just. Socrates suggests that the more evolved a man is, the more he is able to put aside his fears and hankering after comfort and take a stand for his worth and the worth of those he loves. And if necessary, he will form an "alliance for battle with what seems just," even if he "suffers in hunger, cold, and everything of the sort." This quality of courage to take a stand, to fight for one's value, and to be unwilling to make moral compromises is what we call a "spirited commitment to dignity" in the Leadership Dojo. Exemplary leaders embody this commitment.

Over time we have been inspired, motivated, and mobilized by those who are a spirited commitment to dignity. Mother Teresa was committed to the dignity of the disenfranchised, Martin Luther King Jr. to racial equality, the authors of the Declaration of Independence to liberty and justice, Mikhail Gorbachev to the freedom of expression, Rosa Parks to the dignity of the individual, Mahatma Gandhi to individual rights and national sovereignty, the resistance fighters during World War II to religious, ethnic, and racial equality. These individuals created freedoms that we enjoy today because of their dedication and commitment. They are epic examples of people who have changed history by taking a stand for their values. When we think about what we stand for, the scale and impact of these people's efforts may easily daunt us. In comparison we may think our contribution is insignificant and that we can make little difference in the world. It's important to remember that these men and women didn't begin by thinking they were going to change the world. They were people very much like you and me who found themselves passionate about the issues of their time. They committed their resources, skills, and time to solving what they saw as a failure in human interactions. They began by confronting what was in front of them. They also found they were not alone in their concerns; others mobilized around them and large-scale movements began that changed the way we live our lives today. A spirited commitment to dignity is not about being a hero or a martyr, nor is it necessarily about changing the world. Think of those that minister to the sick and dying every day. They won't make the cover of *People* magazine or accumulate great wealth, but they contribute to countless numbers.

EMBODYING A STAND FOR DIGNITY

To live with a spirited commitment to dignity brings one joy, gratitude, power, fulfillment, identity, and a sense of belonging. Many people "think" they are entitled to dignity, and "believe in the right to dignity," but they are not engaged in the embodied practices that produce dignity. A spirited commitment to dignity is different than assuming we are entitled to be treated with dignity simply because we have reached a certain age, created a certain amount of wealth, attained a particular status, or have the legal right to vote. Dignity is not a given; we are not automatically entitled to it. We embody, or become, dignity through a set of practices. Dignity, in other words, is not an ideal or mental construct but an embodiment of what we care about. In the Leadership Dojo, we call this embodying a "stand." When Martin Luther declared, "I can do no other" as he risked his life passing out Bibles to the common man, he was an example of embodying a stand. In that moment his words, actions, and purpose reflected his spirited commitment to dignity.

We make a distinction between embodying a stand and taking a position for a specific reason. When we take a position we live in a shorter horizon of time than when we embody a stand. We take a position when a particular issue is presented to us and we respond to it. We may not have considered the issue previously, but once it comes to our attention we find ourselves taking a position on it. An example would be when the county begins spraying herbicide along your road. You may not be active in environmental affairs, but now you're concerned about the adverse affects this spraying will have on the health of your children, your pets, and the surrounding trees and plants. It may lead to educating yourself about the environmental impact of herbicides and pesticides, to engaging more directly with your local government, mobilizing your neighbors, and attending meetings at city hall. You may even find yourself in a leadership role on this issue. But once there's resolution, or you move to a different city, your concern around this area fades to the background as the other demands of your life take precedent.

An embodied stand, on the other hand, extends over a longer horizon of time. It's a choice we make about what is important over the course of our lives. It's not something we have a passing interest in or are pulled away from by the lure of money, fame, or the next fad. When we embody a stand, we *are* the stand. It's not a thing, issue, or project that is apart from us. Our very identity is the stand. Our passion is the heart of the stand, our thinking is the intention and design of the stand, and our hands and legs take action for the stand. Other issues and situations compete for our interest and time, but what we stand for is always very close to us. An embodied stand becomes a trajectory of purpose.

An example of embodying a stand would be to the health, sustainability, and well-being of our entire global environment. This means that our commitment doesn't end when local issues of our house or neighborhood are resolved. We continue to educate ourselves and others in the importance of environmental sustainability worldwide for our entire lives. We may write op-ed articles for the newspaper, speak at schools, support environmental groups financially and with our services, and live our talk by recycling, buying a hybrid car, and campaigning and voting for this effort. If one

112

embodies this stand, it doesn't end when there's a local success or when one feels personally fulfilled by their actions. To be a stand for the environment means being an active resource in this area for your entire life; it transcends one's ego involvement in the situation. I use this example to illustrate that embodying a stand is a core principle that one lives by. The seduction of money, career, sex, or image doesn't take someone away from his or her stand. An embodied stand is the ground from which you express your spirited commitment to dignity.

There are three distinctions in an embodied stand that are useful in having us take effective action. They are embodying a stand in *language*, embodying a stand in *action*, and *fighting* for your stand.

Embodying a stand in language is the narrative you have about what is important to you. This narrative expresses what you organize your life around. It's the result of reflecting deeply about what matters to you and what you see possible in the historical time that you live. It's not something you have automatically inherited from others, nor is it a novel idea that will bring opportunity your way, nor is it wishful thinking. Embodying a stand in language expresses your values and it produces purpose, meaning, and association with others. When we speak our stand there's no stammering, hesitation, or confusion. Speaking our stand is both a bridge and a boundary in that it builds alliances with some and separates us from others. Our stand will be seen as an invitation to join or as a line that is not to be crossed. Whether others agree or not, they will find us believable, coherent, and committed when we embody a stand in language. We are the embodiment of this narrative.

Embodying a stand in action means that what you do, the activities you're involved in, the actions you take are consistent with what you say. When Gandhi went on his hunger strikes, he embodied his stand; when single mothers work three jobs so their children can have a good education, their actions are the embodiment of a stand; Albert Schweitzer embodied his stand when he went to live in the jungles of Africa to administer to the sick; war protesters are a stand when they march to protest against war. Embodying a stand in action means that we will act wholeheartedly to represent, fulfill, and fight for our stand. It means that our actions maintain integrity with what we say.

Fighting for a stand is the ability to decline what's inconsequential, insist on what's right, require others to pay attention, demand justice, quit those who pull you away from your stand, and, if necessary, put your identity and body at risk for what you say is important. This does not mean reciting a set phrase, mouthing the appropriate words, or posturing in an aggressive manner. It's not an arrogance or self-righteousness about your concerns or "rights." It's not bullying or pushy. It doesn't mean that you're fighting *against* something. It's not an ungrounded emotional reaction because of a slight or because your feelings were hurt. It's putting yourself on the line, and perhaps even in harm's way, in mind, body, and spirit, for what you stand *for*. To fight for your stand requires you to be physically fit, mentally disciplined, emotionally balanced, and morally grounded.

The richness and complexity of our lives require us to navigate among a multiplicity of commitments and concerns. There is, in other words, not simply one stand that we take in our lifetimes. We're called upon to take stands in a number of areas throughout our lives. These universal areas of concern are family, health, job, career, money, identity, play, orientation to life, spirituality, community, education, and avocation.

Exemplary leaders embody their values and what they care about. Committing to practices in language, action, and emotion in which one becomes his or her stand is a mark of exemplary leaders. When we take a stand and fight for what we are about, we produce dignity and self-worth.

In Chapter Six we look at the power of presence for leaders.

Leadership Presence

Recently while doing work on customer service
for a retail chain, I asked employees to visit several
stores. After spending time in many stores, we all
compared notes. To a person, we agreed that we
could "feel" good customer service just walking
into the store. We tried to get more specific by
looking at visual cues, merchandise layouts, facial
expressions—but none that could explain the sure
sense we had when we walked into the store that
we would be treated well. Something else was
going on. Something else was in the air, we could
feel it, we just couldn't describe why we felt it.

Margaret Wheatley, *Leadership and the New Science*

■ ■ ■

I n his groundbreaking book *Silent Messages*, Albert Mehrabian,
professor emeritus of psychology at UCLA, asked the question,
"What makes someone credible?" or "Why do we trust someone?" In his study, people stated that the believability of someone's

message was influenced 7 percent by content, 38 percent by voice tone and tempo, and 55 percent by body language.[1] Variations on this study, which was conducted with two separate audiences over a period of two years, have been replicated numerous times since, with varying populations, by other researchers over three decades. Every study, with only slight differences, arrived at the same results. If we consider that from a somatic perspective, voice tone and tempo fall into the category of body, we can conclude that 93 percent of building trust and credibility is communicated through the body.

This is startling in its frankness; at the same time it intuitively makes sense to us if we inventory our personal experience. Most of us can recall a time when we've moved forward with someone simply because of the way we felt about him or how we sensed him; perhaps there was something about the way he comported himself, however ineffable, that made us trust him and therefore want to interact with him more fully. If we are at all sensitive to the critical importance of trust in human relations, the percentages presented require us to seriously examine their implications. To begin with, they reveal that *how* we are is far more influential and expressive than *what* we're saying. They tell us that our presence *is* language and there is always sensitivity to who we are at a cellular and energetic level. They point out that humans first seek to trust the person rather than the message and that coherence between the message and the person is essential. And from this we can conclude that when we *are* our message, when we *embody* our values, we are at the height of our power and influence. It reveals that our presence, our way of being, is the foundation for building trust, intimacy, and connection with others. In the Leadership Dojo, we say that this presence is the ground upon which exemplary leadership is built.

From a rationalistic standpoint it's easy to fall into the thinking that these percentages refer to the idiom of "body language." That is, if we learn certain techniques and tips we can entice people into believing us by assuming the correct posture. Take for example the numerous leadership formulas that promise a "fast, foolproof, and fun way" of fulfilling on your leadership potential by prescribing the right hair color and style (including the best side to part your hair), correct clothes, speech patterns, gestures, and a step-by-step walk-through in how to handle encounters with those you lead (when they say x you say y). This reductive explanation is based in the Cartesian notion that you could have someone, a salesperson for example, systematically adopt and apply certain behaviors that would put others at ease while the sale is slipped under the radar.

This idea that we can influence others by trying on the right "body language"—as one would try on a fashionable spring coat— trivializes the basic intuition humans have about authenticity and mastery. When we live our lives through tips and techniques we appear inauthentic; we're thought of as lacking substance, as trying too hard to be something we're not. When we see life and others only as a backdrop to our personal dramas, naively thinking that the part can be changed without affecting the whole, or forget that authenticity and purpose emerge from the inside out, we lose the possibility of the ongoing activity of making the world and ourselves anew. The seduction of facile techniques as a means to further certain ends is the Cartesian legacy of control that is effective for manipulating machines but distorts what it's like to work harmoniously with people and animals. This cut-and-paste notion of leadership, or any type of learning for that matter, produces superficial and inauthentic behavior.

There's an indispensable kind of person who cuts a path in the world not simply because of his or her own achievements but because of what he or she has enabled others to achieve. This is a leader who brings focus and energy to a community and helps define the purpose and meaning of living in a particular place and time. This person developed him- or herself not through tips and techniques but through embodying a sensibility about being human. This sensibility is a Leadership Presence rooted in the fundamental skills of embodied practices, respect for life, the cultivation of the self, the primacy of relationship, and a collective vision for living a proper human life. This creates a relationship to the world in which we can take a stand for what we believe in without becoming rigid or fundamentalist and at the same time open our hearts without being sentimental or naïve.

THE PRINCIPLES
OF A LEADERSHIP PRESENCE

In the Leadership Dojo, we say there are five principles that are the ground for a Leadership Presence. These principles are:

1 Centering,

2 Facing,

3 Extending,

4 Entering, and

5 Blending.

Again, we separate these five principles as a convenience for our understanding, but in reality they comprise a unified way of being in the world. Think of centering, facing, extending, entering, and blending as five notes that, if played at the same time, create a chord.

Centering
An embodied commitment to Self-Knowing

> Know thyself.
>
> Socrates

In our office we have a sign on the wall that says, "You Must Be Present to Win." It's taken from a local community raffle ticket, yet it's a profound and ironic reminder of a fundamental truth about leadership and living a life rich with meaning and fulfillment; that is, to be effective in the world it's necessary to be present, to ourselves, others, and the environment. All the great wisdom traditions and perennial philosophies have passed down this timeless truth over the ages. We have all had the experience of standing in front of someone and realizing, often to our horror, that they're not there. Yes, they may have all the appearances of being there, they're appropriately dressed, well groomed, and clearly taking up space, but when you look into their eyes you know it's just a shell that's in front of you. It's difficult to trust and be motivated by someone if they're not present. In fact, a successful way to erode trust is to not be present. Being present through centering is the first step in knowing ourselves at a level deeper than our normal discursive thinking, which is a requisite for exemplary leadership.

Centering is the process of collecting ourselves. It's a way of being with ourselves that brings us present not only to the world but also to what we care about and to our purpose for living. This turn inward is not narcissistic or self-centered but simply means that we attend to what is occurring in the body—the sensations, the emotions, moods, images, and thoughts. This is the first step in the pragmatization of feeling. This is not feeling as sentimentality or self-absorption, but a sensibility that is the foundation for action, relationship, purpose, commitment, and learning. When we become present we gain self-knowledge, which is the first step in leadership. As Sun Tzu, the legendary Chinese general and military strategist said, "First know yourself and then know your enemy."

The process of centering has three distinct stages:

1 Centering in the self,

2 Centering in our commitments, and

3 Centering in spirit.[2]

CENTERING IN THE SELF

In the first stage we bring our attention to the three somatic dimensions of length, width, and depth. This is an alignment of the physical body according to the natural laws of mass, gravity, and posture. This means that we scan to see if we are balanced along our vertical line, top to bottom; horizontal line, left to right; and depth, front to back. If we're aligned along these three dimensions, we're in harmony with the natural law of gravity. This is aligning our energetic field with the gravitational field of the planet. When we're not struggling against gravity, our attention is free to be with others.

We're inwardly calm and outwardly ready for action. We look out at the world from a position of balance and openness. Being comfortable in our own skin helps us builds trust with others.[3]

Practice

To experience this, try this simple practice for centering your physical body.

Stand and align yourself so your head is directly over your shoulders (your ears are directly over the midpoints of the shoulders), your shoulders are over your hips, hips over the knees, and knees over the midpoint of your feet. (This practice can just as easily be done sitting.)

Now relax the eyes. The eyes are connected to the brain by the optic nerve, and if your eyes are rigid and fixed, this will transfer to the brain. The brain will slightly contract, and this tension will precipitate throughout the central nervous system, and thus the entire body. Eye tension may initially be under the level of awareness; if so the entire body will be in a subtle low-grade contraction. This drains us of our vitality and we appear stiff to others. When we relax our eyes, our peripheral vision opens, we see more of life, and we appear more relaxed to others.

Now release the jaw at the hinge and the chin. Our bodies are designed so the teeth never have to touch. When we clamp down on our jaw and gnash our teeth we're usually chewing on something at an emotional or mental level. Notice that when you release your jaw, the breath will also drop. A chronic holding in the jaw is often transferred to the neck, and it can become the cause of neck pain.

Next lift the shoulders and then let them drop as if they're being held by a coat hanger. A natural response to fear is to lift the shoulders, and if we chronically hold our shoulders up we're inviting the emotion of fear. We may not have anything to be afraid of or even think we're afraid of something, but raised shoulders move us toward a fearful experience of life.

Now let the breath drop into the lower abdomen. Our bodies are designed so the breath occurs most naturally and effortlessly in the lower abdomen. In order to do this it's necessary to relax the stomach, which is difficult for most people as the cultural image, derived from movies and magazine covers (the smiling fellow on the cover of *Men's Health* who has that perfect six-pack abs and the airbrushed model on the cover of *Vanity Fair*) conveys the message that a tautly held stomach and a puffed-out chest is the key to beauty. When we do this our breath is high and the organs in the stomach are crowded against each other. When the organs are bunched together in this manner it's more difficult for them to correspond with each other, and this adversely affects our health. This keeps our center of gravity high, which throws us out of balance not only physically, but mentally and emotionally as well.

Now relax the pelvic area and legs. This means releasing the buttocks, anal and genital sphincters, and the muscles in the thighs and calves. This allows the weight of the body to continue to be transferred downward toward the earth. Our system is designed so our bones, not our muscles, hold the weight of our bodies. When we hold ourselves up, away from the earth, by contracting our muscular system, we're exerting far too much energy simply sitting or standing. This contraction away from the earth leaves us ungrounded, which limits our emotional range and ability to build intimacy and trust with others.

Now scan yourself along the horizontal dimension. Sense if you're balanced left to right at the ears, shoulders, hips, and feet. Check to see if your peripheral vision is open so you have a wide vision.

Now scan along the depth of your torso, balancing yourself from front to back so you're not tipped forward into the world, nor are you leaning away from it.

Now drop your attention just below your belly button. This is the center of the three dimensions—your center of gravity. When we move from our center of gravity, the organizing principle of these three dimensions, we're balanced, alert, relaxed, and prepared to take action. Aligning yourself along length, width, and depth is the first stage in centering. When you organize yourself this way—body relaxed, breath dropped, mind free of the dizzying circularity of thought—it's clinically impossible to be anxious.

Right! This is the antidote for anxiety; centering allows us be self-generating and self-healing. Drop your breath, relax, move your attention to sensation and away from thought. Since anxiety is one of the most infectious of moods, because little is accomplished when we're anxious, and because it's difficult to have trusting intimate relationships in this state, the practice of centering has immeasurable value.

When we center in this manner, we inhabit our bodies in a way in which we're relaxed without being slack, and alive and extended without being stiff. This gives us a sense of firmness and weight, and we feel ourselves properly balanced in space. There's a sense of solidity without being fixed; at the same time we have a light touch, because we're more comfortable with ourselves. There's a direct feeling of groundedness when we live inside our bodies this way. We can now deal with the world in a straightforward and confident way. Once we settle into ourselves, we can reflect on what we care about and how we can live our purpose in life. This is a simple yet highly effective practice that is critical for leaders. If we're not centered physically, it's much more difficult to attend to the demands of leadership, and we appear disorganized, lacking a compelling presence, and out of balance.[4]

There's a story from ancient China that illustrates this principle. When a banker would visit a client, the client would have a spy go outside where the shoes were placed and scrutinize the soles of the banker's shoes to see how they were worn. This would tell them if the banker walked in a balanced way, or not, which told them if the banker were also balanced mentally and emotionally and could be trusted with their money.

Practice

After centering, reflect on:

- How did centering shift your mood, thinking, and felt bodily sense?
- What was the primary thing you did with your attention to center? (For example, feel your breath, let go of your jaw, relax your shoulders, soften your gaze, drop your attention to your center of gravity, and so on.)
- How can centering be useful to you as a leader?

CENTERING IN OUR COMMITMENTS

Centering physically doesn't necessarily mean we'll be successful. It means that we're now present to engage with life and have the opportunity to fully play the game of our choice. It's like an ante in a card game; once you pony up your chips you can be dealt cards, but it doesn't guarantee you'll win; it only means you can play. Once we've centered ourselves bodily—that is, become present—we can now center on what matters to us. This can take a number of forms. We can center on a value or a virtue that we want to cultivate, like accountability, patience, or courage. We can center on what we're committed to bringing into the world, like a stronger team, a loving marriage, increased customer satisfaction, a book, or increased sales. Or skills we want to learn, like making stronger declarations, being a better listener, or learning a new piece of technology. In short, it's centering on what we care about, not simply as a wish or desire but as an embodied commitment that will produce observable results. When we center on a commitment, it expands our horizon of time and we open our future.

However, when we begin to commit to a new way of being, it's critical to do so from an embodied state. I have found that when most people center in their commitments without first being grounded in the lived body, the commitment simply devolves into an intriguing idea, a head-trip, fantasy, or hope without any legs under it. These types of individuals simply go from commitment to commitment without manifesting any of them.

The traditional way of committing to something new is to begin by defining what it is we're bringing into form. For example, if it were to be a better listener, we would first define powerful listening. We would then read or hear examples of leaders who were powerful listeners and how this made them effective. We might read a paper or see a PowerPoint presentation that further explained how listening is important for leaders. We would then enter into a discussion in which the students would share their points of view. Finally there may be a reading assignment or keeping a journal of one's progress as a listener. This will reveal the importance of listening, but it will not actually make most of us better listeners or even motivate us to engage in practices to enhance our listening.

From the point of view of the Leadership Dojo, these are just the first steps in learning. While they're important steps, they only set the stage for the embodied learning that allows one to actually take new actions. As I said in Chapter Four, stopping our learning here is a formula for failure. To begin with, there's no commitment to be a better listener with declared benchmarks for improvement and, more importantly, there's no commitment to practice to become a better listener. In addition there's no teacher, coach, mentor, or committed listener to give feedback, keep us on track, celebrate our successes, and help us to learn from our mistakes.

In the Leadership Dojo, we begin where the traditional processes end. After presenting what is to be learned, why it's important to us, and what it looks like, we begin the practices that allow us to fulfill on our vision. This is the critical difference in learning: that is, being able to actually take new actions, distinct from simply collecting new information. This comes from recurrent practices.[5]

CENTERING IN SPIRIT

I'm in an antique store in Tokyo that specializes in rare Samurai weapons. This is not your usual sidewalk retail business—entry is by invitation only; the store caters to serious collectors. I'm tagging along as the guest of an aikido training partner I've made friends with at Hombu Dojo. Besides being a serious martial artist, my friend is a Japanese scholar, a collector of seventeenth-century Samurai weapons, and a longtime resident of Japan. His vouching for me and his credentials admit me into a dusky, heavily locked room at the rear of the store. I browse respectfully while my sponsor converses quietly with the owner. I'm drawn to three swords that sit on a heavily lacquered table. After a time my friend comes over and tells me that the owner says I can handle these swords if I wish. I understand the trust granted to me and I respectfully pick up the first sword, feeling its balance, weight, admiring its workmanship. When I draw the blade out of the sheath I do so with great care, mindful that I assume the correct posture while holding such an extraordinary work of art.

I do the same with the second sword, but when I draw the blade of the third sword I suddenly feel as if I'm holding something alive, like the tail of a writhing boa constrictor, and I must now concentrate as if my hair were on fire. This sword is not simply an inanimate object, a work of art created more than 300 years ago, but something alive and vital, something with a will, an intention of its own. It expresses a living spirit that has a formidable power and I must expand to meet it. Spontaneously my stance opens, seeking a stronger ground, and I extend my energy to meet the power of this impressive weapon. My friend and the owner seem to draw back, as if they too are conscious of a presence that could menace if not properly respected.

I carefully sheath the blade and slowly put it back on the table. I audibly let my breath out and notice the owner smiling curiously. He explains that this sword is from the late Edo period and is different from the other two on the table. The first two, he says, were ceremonial swords and worn primarily in the court. The third, he says, was from the sword maker Kotesu Nagafune and was a battlefield sword recorded to have been responsible for taking more than fifty lives. "This sword," he says, "like others with similar histories, has a spirit of its own. There's a power in it that requires not only respect, but a skill that must transcend the common."

Could what I experienced be measured? Most likely not. Was it observable by others? Perhaps. Would this have been a similar experience for someone else? We don't know. Did the history of the sword justify my experience? It could … or not. Was it a real experience for me? Absolutely. Have others had similar experiences? Throughout human history there have been countless written and oral accounts of individuals and groups being touched by a level of consciousness and energy that we call "Spirit."

The literature on connecting with Spirit—an energy that is beyond the self—through various awareness disciplines is well documented. These include practices such as meditation, martial arts, contemplation, prayer, movement, vision quests, sweat lodges, psychotropic plant medicine, and so on. Or sports like skydiving, downhill skiing, big wave surfing, long-distance swimming and running, horseback riding, triathlons, rock climbing, and such. There are numerous accounts of individuals who have had near-death episodes, life-threatening accidents, illnesses, or moments of intense trauma that create a heightened awareness revealing the presence of Spirit. Indigenous people, across time and across cultures, have practices that centralize Spirit in their lives and cosmology. Often this state of consciousness will simply befall someone without the person consciously engaging in any activity at all or with any particular intention.

From a somatic perspective, Spirit is a felt bodily state. It's an embodiment of a state of consciousness in which the attributes of depth, connection, power, being, unity, wholeness, and love are directly experienced. It's a process, not an end state, in which one is moved and informed by a power called *energy, ki, chi, élan vital, prana, shabd,* depending on the language of your culture. This energy is experienced as larger than the self, yet includes it and is accompanied by humility and awe at the mystery of life. When the body is touched by the energy of Spirit, the "I" we normally think of as our self no longer holds center stage; thus the heightened experience of depth and connection has a more universal feeling about it, even though we are more personally present and intimate with the world. Life is filled with more order and meaning, even though the normal "me" is not making meaning and order.

The embodied experience of Spirit ties our common sense in knots—we're in choice, but out of control; disorganized, but stable; still while in movement; knowing without understanding; listening without ears; surrendering to be victorious; giving in to succeed; dying to live. This paradox of embodied Spirit is often described in terms of grace, awe, unity, reverence, presence, wonder, and beauty.

Exemplary leaders center on Spirit in order to contact the perennial wisdom that informs the self.

We do this not by leaving or transcending the body but by descending deeper into it. Deep within our living body is the genesis of an ethical and moral sustainability of life that is grounded in compassion and wisdom. Contacting this deep energy connects us to an intelligence that informs our actions in a way that's not possible in our normal state of cognition. For leaders to attain a perspective that's beyond the self, they need to be in practices that put them in relationship with Spirit. As philosopher Henri Bergson writes, "The intellect is characterized by a natural inability to know life."

The extraordinary story of Pius Mau Piailug exemplifies this phenomenon of Spirit as a deep energy that informs our lives. In 1976 the National Geographic Society asked Piailug, one of the last surviving old-time navigators, to demonstrate how centuries ago people navigated over the open ocean without modern technology. In a replica of an ancient canoe, he sailed 2,500 miles across the Pacific Ocean, from Hawaii to Tahiti, using the old ways. He explained that he navigated in part by using what he called a "star compass," which he illustrated by placing thirty-two pieces of coral in a circle; he then retraced the rising and setting of each star. He also said that if it was too cloudy to see the stars, he could read a complex map of waves through eight sets of swells. When asked what he did if it was too dark or foggy to see the swells, he explained that he would lie down in the bottom of the voyager canoe and *feel* the waves and therefore set a course by what he *felt* in his body. He said he could *feel* the essence of each wave.

Feel a wave that bounced off a land mass 2,000 miles away and navigate correctly by it! It boggles the mind that one can draw on an intelligence that is beyond cognition and intuition and lives in all of us as a possibility. This level of pragmatic wisdom is the exact point of the importance of Spirit in building exemplary leaders. The following poem by Chuang Tzu, written more than 2,000 years ago, again exemplifies how contacting the deep energy of Spirit brings forward a skillful and informed action that's not possible with only the rational mind.

> Prince Wan Hui's cook
> Was cutting up an ox.
> Out went a hand,

Down went a shoulder,
He planted a foot,
He pressed with a knee,
The ox fell apart
With a whisper,
The bright cleaver murmured
Like a gentle wind.
Rhythm! Timing!
Like a sacred dance,
Like "The Mulberry Grove,"
Like ancient harmonies!
"Good work!" the Prince exclaimed,
"Your method is faultless!"
"Method?" said the cook
Laying aside his cleaver,
"What I follow is Tao
Beyond all methods!
"When I first began
To cut up oxen
I would see before me
The whole ox
All in one mass.
"After three years
I no longer saw this mass.
I saw the distinctions.
"But now, I see nothing
With the eye. My whole being
Apprehends.
My senses are idle. The Spirit

133

Free to work without plan
Follows its own instinct
Guided by natural line,
By the secret opening, the hidden space,
My cleaver finds its own way.
I cut through no joint, chop no bone.
"A good cook needs a new chopper
Once a year—he cuts.
A poor cook needs a new one
Every month—he hacks!
"I have used this same cleaver
Nineteen years.
It has cut up
A thousand oxen.
Its edge is as keen
As if newly sharpened.
"There are spaces in the joints;
The blade is thin and keen:
When this thinness
Finds that space
There is all the room you need!
It goes like a breeze!
Hence I have this cleaver nineteen years
As if newly sharpened!
"True, there are sometimes
Tough joints. I feel them coming,
I slow down, I watch closely,
Hold back, barely move the blade,
And whump! The part falls away

Landing like a clod of earth.
"Then I withdraw the blade,
I stand still
And let the joy of the work
Sink in.
I clean the blade
And put it away."
Prince Wan Hui said,
"This is it! My cook has shown me
How I ought to live
My own life!"[6]

The lines,

My whole being / Apprehends. / The Spirit / Free to work without plan / Follows its own instinct / Guided by natural line, / By the secret opening, the hidden space, / My cleaver finds its own way

speak to the innate intelligence of Spirit that creates skillful action. This notion is recounted in the stories of the martial artist who waits until the perfect moment to stop his opponent with a single glance or the acupuncturist who needs only to place a single needle, instead of a dozen, to heal her patient, the horsewoman who with only the most subtle motion can transform the unruly horse into an engaged partner, the leader who walks into a room and immediately knows the way to resolve the conflict on the team, the general who neutralizes the enemies' strength without undue force.

It's true that competency is developed through years of training and experience; it's also true that technique and training alone do not accomplish mastery. The step from competency to mastery requires that we open to an energy greater than our personality and learned techniques. This energy is what we call "Spirit."

It's necessary for exemplary leaders to be centered in the deep energy of Spirit. In fact it may be more important than centering in the self and centering in commitments because more than ever leaders need to embody the responsibility of the spiritual dimension of their role and not simply be locked into quarterly profits and shareholder pressures. This spiritual dimension includes environmental awareness, social justice, gender equity, class and race consciousness, realizing purpose and talent in the workplace, holding conflict as a generative force, envisioning a future in which ethics and morality lead to an inner harmony and a society of cooperation. These are all issues that the energy of Spirit can help bring into reality.

But first it's important that we ground ourselves in the body before centering in Spirit. Without first grounding somatically, people often hold Spirit as simply a good idea and not a direct, lived experience. If we don't center first in the body we're too likely to go off into la-la land and live only in the *concept* of energy and Spirit. Embodiment makes Spirit direct, applicable, and real.

To invoke the energy of Spirit, the key principle is to remember that whatever practice one chooses it's in the service of contacting Spirit. Recall the parable of the stonecutters in which the activity of stonecutting is connected to building a cathedral. Whatever practice we choose, either of our own invention, given to us by a teacher, or acquired from a long-standing tradition, has the purpose of connecting us to the energy of Spirit. This means that we consciously intend to have a larger energy enter into us through our practice of choice.

Practices

- Choose a place where you invoke the energy of Spirit. This can be a place in your house, office, or in nature. You can infuse it with meaning by burning a candle, having an object of power like a stone, photo, small statue, plant, floral arrangement, painting, or drawing. Whatever it is, make it meaningful to you and aesthetically pleasing. When you enter into this space, acknowledge that you're now consciously invoking the power of Spirit.

- Center yourself with the intention of moving from the thinking self to the feeling, sensing self. You can do this in a sitting practice, walking practice, or movement practice. Feel yourself along length, width, and depth. Drop your attention to your stomach center and your heart center. Remember that what's important is the commitment to open yourself to an energy that is deeper and more connected than that of the thinking self.

- What do you feel and sense when you open to the energy of Spirit? What is its quality or essence? How does it move you? If you gave it a voice, what would it be saying to you?

- Why is connecting with Spirit important to you as a leader?

Facing

An embodied commitment to Integrity

> The supreme quality for leadership is unquestionably integrity. Without it, no real success is possible, no matter whether it is on a section gang, a football field, in an army, or in an office.
>
> Dwight D. Eisenhower

Somewhere between eight and twelve months old, we go through a thorough and profound transformation that forever changes who we are; moreover, it's a change that we continue to enact on a daily basis.

We stand.

And we begin to stand up for ourselves.

When we stand we shape ourselves in a way that is not possible for any other animal. Standing frees our hands to grip and handle, our torso and genitals are exposed to the world, we see further because our head rests on top of our spine and we are able to face directly into the world.

Every time we stand we reenact the moment when our early ancestors stood and became *Homo sapiens*. We live the story of our species every morning when we rise out of bed. To be upright and face the world is an evolutionary moment in which we embody the human capacity for choice; we are asked to be equal to this challenge every day. When we literally face the world, we come face to face with choosing how to live our lives. Through the literal and metaphorical aspect of facing we are given the opportunity to choose how we move into the future. While centering is a commitment to be in the game of life, facing is a commitment to a specific aspect of our life: a situation, a conversation, an enterprise, a person, task, relationship, or unresolved issues.

No surprise that when we speak of someone as "upright" or "having a spine" or "taking a stand for what's right" or "able to face the situation" or "forward looking" or she "holds her head up proudly" or "holds himself tall" or "keeps her chin up," we're commenting on the individual as an honorable and morally mature person. In this way facing is a commitment to integrity; facing is a choice to engage and confront what is necessary for an ethical and moral outcome.

When we first consider this notion of facing, we're momentarily taken aback. Our common sense tells us that of course we face. How could we not? We are face to face with people and events all the time. Our eyes are in the front of our face. Yet we when we look closely we see that there are certain situations and people that we do not truly square off to and face.

Practice

Go to public places where people gather—coffee shops, stores, cafés, malls, parks, museums, and so on—and see how the people face or align to each other, or not. Notice how heads are cocked to one side, questioning, or meekly bowed, or lifted arrogantly, shoulders turned away indifferently, eyes averted, a dismissal with the chin in a greeting, an apologetic caving in.

Or notice how people turn toward each other, look each other in the eye, directly face who or what they're looking at.

- What impression is made when people do not face?
- What impression is made when people are facing?
- As a leader, what did you learn from this practice?

Notice how difficult it is for most young children to face adults or difficult situations. For most of them it's almost impossible to make sustained eye contact or to fully align their bodies to the encounter. This is not an inherent fault but points to the fact that facing is a developmental skill that is learned. Children who are not taught to face others and themselves become the adults who shy away from difficult situations, are conflict averse, or compensate by being belligerent and pushy.

Now observe how you are with others and how they are with you. What are the ways in which others do not face you, and what assessment does that produce in you? What are the ways you do not face others or challenging situations? What is the sensation of avoiding or not facing? That is, when you avoid a conversation or confrontation with someone, how does that feel in your body? Do you squeeze your stomach, deaden your eyes, turn subtly away, bite down on your teeth, or invent a story that justifies why you don't have to engage? By noticing what we do in our bodies, we have a more direct access to our mental and emotional state and therefore more choice about shifting it.

It's a crucial skill for leaders to face into life with directness, authenticity, and compassion. When we truly align and face, we see who's there, not just our idea of who we think should be there, or how they should be, or a socially constructed idea of someone, but the person who is actually in front of us. Facing brings us into a direct relationship with what is occurring instead of wishing or hoping it to be some way other than it is. Facing gets us out of our heads and allows us to see what needs to get done, with whom, and how to do it. When we face, we reduce the pull of the past and the compulsion of the future, and we're able to be present in the moment. After we center, we can face those issues that call for action.

Facing also means facing ourselves. When we face ourselves we engage in the questions of meaning, integrity, purpose, legacy, and calling. This has to do with looking sincerely at what it is that fulfills

140

us, about fully using our talents and gifts, committing to a life of our choosing, being honest with ourselves and with others, and taking a stand for what's important to us.

When we authentically face, we engage others and situations in a direct and purposeful manner. When we do not face, we avoid the courageous conversations; we're inauthentic, dishonest, or we procrastinate taking action. If we're not facing something in ourselves it will be reflected in how we are in the world; and what we're avoiding in the world will have its counterpoint in what we're avoiding in ourselves. David's story illustrates the principle of facing and how internal and external challenges are often connected.

David asked for help in forming his new group into a high-participating, cooperative, self-generating team. At the time, he was the senior vice president of human resources of a large multinational corporation and was five years away from retiring. His office walls and shelves were full of awards and plaques in recognition of his successful career. David was at the top of his game and he was seen as a powerful, decisive, and committed leader. But a strange phenomenon began to appear as we engaged in the conversations about individual and team purpose. In speaking about what he truly stood for, David began to fold in on himself, his usual steady eye contact wavered, and his voice dropped to a whisper. When I asked him about what legacy he wanted to leave, his body would slightly turn away. These gestures were all fairly subtle to the common eye, but to someone who is trained to notice them, they were a cue that there was something he was avoiding, something he wasn't facing, that was reflected through his body. When I pointed this out to him, he was at first surprised, and then as he became aware of it, he began to open to what his body was revealing.

"For the past couple of years," he began, "I've known that what I really want to do is to influence the company's culture in a way in which people will say, 'Being in this organization was a turning point in my life. What I learned here helped me become the person that I am now, both personally and professionally.' This kind of growth is what I think is important for the success of the people, and the company, and I have an idea about how it can be done."

He went on, "I've had a successful career and I've enjoyed immensely what I've done, but it's no longer enough. More and more I feel like all I'm doing is the technical work of my job and not helping people in the way that I know that I can. I work with good people, I make good money, I'm grateful for all that. But it's flat; it's no longer interesting. There's no juice in it anymore and I know I can do more … and I want to."

As he spoke he began to lengthen into his full posture, he turned toward me and fixed me with his gaze. It was clear he was now fully facing what he cared about.

When I asked him why he didn't act on his vision, his shoulders rounded and he glanced away. He appeared to be thinking about something that puzzled him, something that maybe he could never make sense of, as if he were imprisoned by the thought of whatever it was. This change of comportment was subtle, but it was significant. "I haven't said this to anyone except my wife."

He paused and looked back at me, "I'll be honest with you. I'm afraid that if I implement this kind of transformation, it'll threaten my position. What I have in mind is a sea change, and it could endanger my career and my retirement package. It's difficult for me to say, and I'm not proud of it, but I'm afraid of taking the risk."

David and I spent time with the tension between what he wanted to do and how he perceived it would negatively affect the status quo—his and the company's. It became clear that for some time David hadn't been fully facing what mattered to him at this stage in his life and it was draining his passion and vitality. This was an increasing weight on him, as he had lost his purpose and trajectory in life. The situation was further complicated because he felt ashamed that he was paralyzed by fear and isolated because he hadn't shared how much he cared about this.

When I asked him if he had brought this up with his boss he shook his head. "There are a number of times I've decided to talk to him, but when I get in front of him, I just balk; I can't do it. It's unlike me, but I get tongue-tied and then he brings up another issue and I just let it slide." When he spoke of this, his body bowed and he again subtly turned away.

The point at which David knew what he wanted to do but found he was incapable of taking the necessary action is pivotal in embodied learning. It's the difference between knowing and acting. It's assumed that when we have an insight we should easily be able to transform it into a behavior. In truth most people are unable to take insight into immediate action. What is required is a time of practice so the insight can be embodied. Insights, which are important, live in the cognitive domain; action lives in the body. Because we're taught, and then assume, that insight is the end goal, it's not uncommon that we fall into shame and guilt when we can't act on our insights. When we're captured by these emotions, our energy, time, and attention go into managing the shame instead of taking action. A primary premise of the Leadership Dojo is that new practices are required to take new actions. When we fully comprehend this, we gracefully allow the time to practice so that we can embody new behaviors.

Facing is a practice that allows us to encounter the world and ourselves in a direct, unmediated manner. For David to encounter his changing inner world it was necessary that he take on new practices. His first practice was to continue speaking about his vision and desire to move his professional life into new directions. This practice included aligning his body so he was directly facing the person to whom he was talking. When he found himself contracting or drifting away, his practice was to center and face.

Second, his daily solo practice was centered on facing the issues that he had voiced around contribution and legacy. He would begin his daily practices by reminding himself of the importance of engaging in these issues and speaking them to the appropriate people. He would then do his somatic practices—sitting and running—and when he finished he would again remind himself why he did the practice.

Third, he committed to the practice of speaking his new offer to his boss. In the beginning it didn't matter if he was able to do it or not; it was simply important that he engage in the process and observe how he was in it. In other words, even if he wasn't successful he could observe how he stopped himself in word, mood, emotion, and action. Even if he became tongue-tied, he began to see how he did this to himself. This increased his choice and opened new possibilities for him. When he would fall into his old pattern, he recognized his paralysis earlier and was able to recenter and engage his vision freshly.

Over time David became centered in what this stage in his life required. He found that he was willing to take the risk of saying what he felt was needed for the success of the employees and the company and to fulfilling his purpose in life. To his surprise, his boss readily accepted the idea and said that he too had been thinking along these lines but was a bit reluctant to voice it.

Practices

- What are the difficult or "courageous conversations" that you find yourself avoiding?

- Center and make a commitment to face these conversations, situations, or people.

- Center your solo practice on facing what you're avoiding.

- Note what happens in your body—mood, sensations, and stories—when you face the difficult conversations.

- When you get thrown off center, return to center and continue to face into what is required.

- Choose a tree, a pole, or some marker, and stand about thirty feet away, facing it. Center, face this object directly, and think of it as that person or situation you need to face and then walk directly toward it in a centered manner. When you arrive, touch it with your hand. Notice how this feels in your body. Notice when you waver or are captured by negative thoughts. Then recenter and do the practice again.

- How does facing make you a more powerful leader?

Extending

An embodied commitment to Listening

Energy follows attention.

Cybernetic axiom

Once we center and face, we can now extend our attention toward that which requires our care. Extending our attention produces a level of perception that enhances connection and communication. Energy follows attention, and this energy provides a channel, much like a radio wave, in which we are able to sense into a situation that goes beyond our customary way of perceiving. A hallmark of exemplary leaders is the ability to "read between the lines," to attend deeply to the concerns, intentions, motivations, desires of others. In this way extension is a commitment to deep listening.

Our attention is not confined to the sense organs for sight, smell, hearing, tasting, and touch. Our attention is like a sixth organ that can be honed and strengthened like a muscle.[7] This is *synaesthesia,* the synthesis of all the senses as they align and function together to create the organ of attention. We can concentrate our attention like a laser beam into a highly concentrated focus, or open it to take in a wide horizon. We can move our attention within to our own sensations, our thinking, and internal images, as well as externally to the environment, people, and the world. Think of the hunters of old whose senses were refined and far reaching; they could perceive the smallest nuance as well as take in the largest view possible. While sensuously communicating with the life pulsing about them they could pick out the hidden anomaly. Our success and fulfillment as leaders depends to a great deal on how we organize, intend, and extend our attention.

When our attention is fragmented we feel unmoored, direction-less, and lacking purpose; our awareness of others, the environment, and ourselves becomes severely limited. When our attention is shaped and embodied by conscious intent, we create depth and connection. To fulfill on our pledge as leaders, it's essential to know what to attend to and how to extend our attention toward that end.

Energy follows attention. What we put our attention on will appear more vivid in our field of our awareness.

Practice

Try this: Place your attention on the breath as it moves in and out of your nose. Now place your attention on the sounds around you. Now place your attention on your sit bones as they meet the chair. Now place your attention on a loved one who is not with you. If you did this you noticed that wherever you directed your attention, the sensations, sounds, feelings, thoughts, and images of that place or person emerged to the foreground of your awareness. Your attention increased your awareness of this area and allowed you to interact with it and make choices concerning it. All the other phenomena were still occurring—the breath, sounds, the sensation of sitting, the image of a loved one—but what you placed your attention on came to life and you were able to distinguish its finer shadings and give it meaning. Charles Darwin said, "Attention or conscious concentration on almost any part of the body produces some direct physical effect on it."

From a somatic point of view the extension of our attention is intimately linked with perception, communication, and imagination.

When we extend our attention toward someone we become informed about who that person is in the world—his or her attributes, motivations, intention, and qualities of being. When our conscious attention touches someone and informs our perceptions, there's a dynamic interplay, a reciprocal encounter at a very intimate level, between the perceiver and the perceived. Extending in this manner is both touching and being touched. It makes us part of who we're communicating with. We touch someone with our attention and they feel touched by it, and touching them touches us. In other words, perception at this level is not a logical calculation but a gregarious participation in the world in which our imagination lends itself to making meaning and direction.

Imagination is a core element in extending our energy. In our usual way of thinking, imagination is considered fantasy, whimsy, or daydreaming; something trivial, as expressed in, "That's only your imagination," or "You're only imagining that." But more than a century ago, the English poet and philosopher Samuel Coleridge made the distinction between fancy and imagination when he said, "Imagination is a faculty of the soul." The Romantic poet John Keats referred to the "Truth of the Imagination." From a somatic point of view, imagination is not a mental construct but an attribute of synaesthesia. Imagination as an extension of our energy goes beyond what each individual sense is capable of in order to connect with those things we do not directly sense and makes it possible to touch the invisible or hidden aspects of a situation or person. In this way we bring forward a world and form an image of that which is not yet visible or present in the normal sense of time. We open our horizons of what is possible and begin the process of creating the future itself.

Consider animals that extend their attention through their senses over great distances, like the eagle that can see a rabbit in detail over a mile away, your family dog that can not only distinguish smells at great distances but can smell emotions like fear at length, the owl that can hear a mouse in a foot of snow a quarter of a mile away, or whales that send and receive sonar signals over 2,000 miles, or the master martial artist who can sense the move of an opponent even before the person begins to move.

Practice

Try this: Stand and center yourself. Extend your right arm in front of you parallel to the ground. Relax your shoulder, elbow, and wrist without going slack. Extend your attention out your arm, palm, and fingers. Now imagine that your attention, or energy, *ki, chi, élan vital, prana,* whatever word you use to name it, is moving beyond your arm and hand and goes through the wall in front of you into the far distance. Now imagine that you can extend it to the corners of the universe. Have a partner try to bend your arm. If you continue to extend your energy and imagine it going to a great distance you'll see that it's impossible for your partner to bend your arm, however hard they try, and you're able to do so without effort.

This is an example of the interplay among attention, energy, and imagination. By feeling how you're self-organizing in this state, it's possible to replicate it without having to take a particular position, like having your arm up. In other words, you can extend your attention out into the world or deep into yourself by simply directing your attention without moving your physical body. Try doing this with your gaze so your eyes are relaxed but extended, and imagine that your attention, through your eyes, is literally touching what you see. You can also do this with your breath, your heart energy, or from your *hara,* your center of gravity.

While it's a birthright to be able to sense someone to this degree, most people don't extend because they are either too self-absorbed or they're fearful of a level of contact and intimacy that goes deeper than surface level. It's also important not to overextend and leave one's body in the desire to make contact. When we overextend we're either looking too far outside of ourselves for approval or we're not firmly anchored in our own bodies—our own experience—and suddenly find ourselves lost in another's experience or value system without consciously intending to do so.

The story of Cesilee is an unusual account of the power of extending.

Ces, as she is called, is the executive director of the Washington Initiative for Supported Employment, a nonprofit in Seattle whose mission is "partnering with communities to promote employment for people with disabilities through innovation and change." Her efforts have helped Washington State's business community, in partnership with local organizations and government agencies, to become a national leader in creating employment opportunities for adults with developmental disabilities. Her role puts her into contact with a wide variety of people from the disabled to CEOs of major firms to politicians and government leaders.

While she's enjoyed a successful career as a social leader, she's also been a world-class athlete. She was a college softball and basketball player and currently plays shortstop for the Seattle Express.

The summer of 2005, the Seattle Express won the Women's A World Series slow pitch softball title of the USSSA (United States Specialty Sports Association) in Panama City, Florida. Ces was the World Series MVP and she was inducted into the Washington State USSSA Hall of Fame in the fall of 2006.

There are many more awards, honors, and titles to Ces's credit, but she never speaks about her athletic prowess unless directly asked, and you have to dig hard to get that. She's more diminutive in stature than large, and sitting quietly at the back of the room works fine for her until she can add value; but when she does speak, she has clout and people listen to her. Her freckled nose and straw-colored hair make you think of the girl next door who might be a cheerleader instead of an All-Star shortstop or point guard. All this is immediately transformed the moment she picks up a bat or throws a ball; the bar instantly goes up, and if you're not prepared to go the distance with her, you should sit back down.

Ces attended the Leadership Dojo to further her professional development but when she returned home she found she was hitting the ball thirty feet further. When her coach asked her what she had been doing she said, "I'm centered now."

He looked at her quizzically, "What's that?"

Her playing improved the more she practiced the somatic work, and at the same time changes began to appear in her professional life as well. In her own words: "I honestly believe that my athletic and professional selves are in the midst of a meld. I employ an athletic approach to my professional role. I practice, I compete, I lead, I follow, and I create every day at work just like I do in my sport. I have many more years as an athlete than as an executive, so my awareness of change in myself is often more pronounced on the playing field. What I learn and experience from the playing field is then transferred into my professional role.

"As an athlete I condition my physical and mental self through the practices of the sport. My mental practices are woven into the physical practices to enhance the opportunity for success during games. I work with a predetermined set of emotions to maximize the potential of the physical self to create the proper way of being for the sport. This then becomes the way I see my opponent as well. I have spent years watching my competitors to gather information on their weaknesses and strengths through my assessment of their physical and mental capacities. Then, on the playing field, I try to exploit their weaknesses and keep them from playing into their strengths; unless we had compatible strengths and then I would employ the notion of 'beating them at their own game.'

"This framework has worked fairly well for me in my athletic career. But, what I've discovered in somatics has added new depth, consistency, power, and passion to my athletic performance. What I've learned is that my entire emotional self is in play too. That is, if I extend toward my opponent, my teammates, and my coaches, like I learned in the somatic work, I'll know more about them and thus be able to begin a new relationship with them. This is what I believe happened in the World Tournament in 2005. As I began to focus my attention on moods, feelings, history, intentions, and what motivated my opponents I began to see them as whole persons. This is very different than seeing the opposing pitcher through a fixed lens.

"As I shifted my perception, my own desires shifted. I shifted from beating my opponent to sharing with my opponent. I was still noticing weaknesses and openings but now I was doing it to connect to them rather than exploit, avoid, or battle them. I began to be with my opponents in a new way and it caused a major shift in me internally and in my external performance. I was more calm, balanced, and confident. I was centered in my role and was able to stay grounded in my own abilities and enjoy myself. I still wanted the same outcome—"the win"—but in the win my attention was on my opponent and teammates in a different way. I now realize that even in competition we're in relationship together and that the time together on the field has the potential to influence our understanding of each other in a way I had never thought of before.

"In this new learning, I was able to achieve new performance outcomes throughout the season. But I knew something had shifted significantly when I first stepped into the batter's box in the World Championship game. I had gone through my typical routines to prepare myself and when I stepped up to the plate I turned slightly toward the pitcher so I could extend toward her, feel her energy, and look for a new opening. These subtle shifts of my body, which included attention and extension, created a new batting stance. My old stance blocked out what instinctually felt right. In my new stance, I felt a new confidence. I saw a new opening. I had been attempting to beat this pitcher at her game for years and she had consistently stopped me. In the off-season, I had gone away and tried to develop more muscle, practice my batting swing more, and visualize the perfect result so I could hit her the next time I faced her. Yet, what I felt at that moment was a sense of ease. I had finally found the opening that I had been looking for over the past seasons. The opening I saw was her area of concern rather than her weakness. I felt that it was important to send the ball back to her with this new information. As the ball went by her I ran to first base elated. It seemed way too easy and yet I was standing on base and she was staring at me with a new level of respect."

Incidentally, at the end of the game she approached me and said inquisitively, "You're doing something different. What is it?"

"I'll tell you when the series is over," and we laughed together.

"Through this new connection we would elevate each other's game and therefore elevate the sport. There would still be a winner and loser, but we would also have the larger product of beautifying our sport. This shift allows the athletic competition to become an expression of power, grace, and beauty. Remember: same sport, same physical and mental training, but very different outcome.

"I now take the same approach each day in my professional role. My organization is working on the issue of unemployment of adults with developmental disabilities. Approximately 75 percent of adults with developmental disabilities in the United States are unemployed. The task is large but we can extend toward and connect with our competition in this area as well. We just shift from the softball field to the business community, my coworkers, the board of directors, individuals with disabilities, and the community at large. By extending to these stakeholders I can now attend to moods, feelings, history, concerns, and visions in new and deeper ways. And, the win is now providing opportunities to others and allowing new expressions of power, grace, beauty, and possibility to come from this particular part of our population. I see how my ability to lead my organization in this effort is anchored in my ability to extend myself and deepen my ability to attend to the environment on multiple levels.

"As I grow in my leadership, I shift my old conditioned behaviors and I tinker with my ability to extend myself on behalf of my organization and the people we represent. I'm starting to experience more calm, balance, and confidence in my leadership. I connect with people more readily and more deeply and I enjoy them more and they know it. I'm still in the beginning phases of challenging the limits in the business we're in, but I've seen it work on the playing field. I have every confidence that I will see new amazing "wins" in the business game. "The ability to extend allows me the opportunity to transcend my historical limitations and demonstrate my passions and bring to reality my personal vision. I ponder my development as a leader and as a human being every day. I wrestle with letting my thoughts hide my feelings rather than letting my feelings inform my thoughts. I continue to see great results when I turn into the experience, extend myself, and settle my attention into the opportunity before me. Now I have both a World Championship and an MVP title that required defeating the best pitcher in our country to remind me how amazing we all can be if we continue to develop our attention muscle and extend thoughtfully into the world. Stay tuned for more stories later!"

Ces's story is a powerful reminder that by extending on the playing field of sports and life, we can build new relationships and new futures for others and ourselves. I'm reminded of Winston Churchill when he said, "Waterloo was won on the playing fields of Eton."

Practices

- Do the extension practice with your arm extended out from a centered position as described earlier in this section. Notice what this extension feels like in your arm—the sensations, the shape, the sense of it. Stay relaxed without being slack and extended without being stiff. Now feel or imagine that same quality of extension along the long muscles next to your spine, in your eyes and your gaze, in your breath, in the energy coming from your chest and heart.

- Extend toward some object like a tree, a plant, or a stone. What does it feel like to "touch" this object with your attention? What information do you pick up about its qualities, its state of being, the nature of its essence?

- In conversation with someone, extend toward them so they feel you're fully with them. While centered and facing, allow your attention to rest on the other. What information do you pick up about their state of being, a quality of being, or the nature of their essence?

- How are you touched when you extend out to touch someone or something?

- How does extending make you a more powerful leader?

Entering
An embodied commitment to *Courage*

> He who has found and knows his soul has found all the world.
> *The Upanishads*

Imagine this: Recently you find yourself annoyed by a colleague. Nothing big—a borrowed book lost, late to a few appointments, negative moods—but he increasingly irritates you. You begin to second-guess yourself; perhaps you're the one who's become ungenerous and short in temperament. But his behavior continues; others notice the same thing, yet you're reluctant to talk to him.

A low-level dread overtakes you when his name appears on your phone caller ID. You're stiff around him; you avoid him, and it begins to affect your working relationship. When you bring this up to your partner at home, he or she is matter of fact in encouraging you to raise the subject, as if it's a common issue of little consequence. Logically this makes sense, but you are mysteriously unsure of yourself in confronting him. You decide to go forward, so you mentally rehearse what you're going to say and justify why you're bringing it up. It all seems very straightforward, and you've recovered a sense of forthrightness about yourself. But when the moment arrives you find yourself hesitating, momentarily paralyzed; time slips by and you part ways without saying what you intended. Over time your irritation increases, but you bury it and the tension burns in your stomach. One day you blow up over an insignificant incident with him. He looks at you askance, people are alarmed, and they now begin to wonder about you.

Over the years I've heard countless renditions of this story and have lived it myself. That is, when it comes time to engage in difficult encounters we find ourselves backing out no matter how much we intellectually understand what we have to do and why we're doing it. This is the moment of entering, and I hope that what I've made clear from my example is that it's not simply an intellectual insight but something that is required of the body. While it makes perfect sense for us to engage in the "courageous conversations," at the end of the day it's not perfect sense that makes it happen. What gets the job done is putting our bodies in front of the necessary person or situation and speaking directly and authentically to them. This takes practice and is a necessary leadership skill that can be learned.

157

In aikido there's a move called *irimi*, which means entering.[8] Irimi is when you enter into the heart of the attack. In aikido we train ourselves this way because we consider that a solution to a problem may be in the problem itself, or the resolution of an attack may be in the energy of the attack itself. This entering move is not to oppose the attack but to move to the center of it, blend with its energy, and resolve it in a nonviolent way. This is not a soft-minded approach but an extremely effective form of self-defense. This has a clear and present application to how we lead in our personal and professional lives.

Irimi is a strong, highly committed move that is not done as a mindless charge forward but as way of engaging with a situation to resolve it creatively. We first *center* ourselves so we're physically, emotionally, and spiritually balanced; we sort out what we need to *face;* we *extend* our attention toward it to gather information and form a relationship with it; and then we *enter* to engage in a responsible, direct way that moves the action forward. Think of entering, or irimi, as a movement toward life that's based in wisdom and compassion, not hope or fantasy.

When we enter in this way we're declaring, "I am here to engage with you in a responsible, ethical manner. I come in a spirit of choice and collaboration. I acknowledge this is a risk for both of us, but I'm committed to moving us toward a mutuality of maturity, connection, and power."

Practice

Try this: Have a partner extend his or her arm toward your chest and then walk directly toward you. (This is the same move I described in the *rondori* practice in Chapter Four.) Notice what your conditioned tendency is. Do you fade back, go in your head, lean forward to fight, hold your breath, become defensive? As your partner comes close, step toward their outstretched hand and then slide off the line of their approach at the last moment so you are next to them but have not interrupted their movement. Consciously connecting this physical practice to the individual or situation you need to enter toward in your life trains your body to directly engage with them. In other words, have your training partner who is coming toward you represent that person or situation in your life. You can even give them a line to speak to you in order to add vividness to the practice, such as, "I don't think I can get the job done like you asked." And you can formulate a response such as, "This is unacceptable. You have to be accountable for your actions."

The stage of entering was central for Norman's evolution as a person and as a leader.

"I'm just not sure I can work with him anymore," Norman would tell me, slowly shaking his head as if to rid himself of the thought. "It's that he's . . ." He would catch himself in mid-sentence and then start again, "Well, I just don't know if I can go on with him this way." His voice would trail off, his eyes scouring the floor as if the next thought was lying in wait around his feet. Norman's docility in the face of conflict prevented him from taking the necessary steps to a fulfilling professional life.

Norman is on the shortlist to be the chief financial officer of a new division of a Fortune 50 company. He's been in the company nearly his entire career and through hard work, consistent success, and a good attitude he's made it to this professional rung. He's deliberate, without noise or excess, and the people on his teams unfailingly speak favorably of him. You would trust him with your money; if it were your firm, you would trust him with the company's money. He's extraordinarily bright, a superior financial analyst, yet his boss, though recommending him for the position, publicly berates him. He wants Norman to have more presence during meetings but humiliates him when he offers a perspective different than his own. When I asked Norman for an example of what his boss would say, it was beyond discourteous and into the offensive. As bad as this was, it was more shocking that Norman would tolerate this behavior, either in public or private, for so long. Norman feels he's earned this new position and can be successful in it, but he's in serious consideration about whether he's willing to continue to work under this boss.

What was missing in this equation was that Norman never confronted his boss about his colossally rude behavior. When I asked him about this, he simply shrugged and said he had tried. With some digging, I found out that *tried* meant asking his boss questions that he hoped might make him reflect on his behavior. When I pointed out that asking questions was different than asking for what you wanted, he nodded submissively, without commitment. He understood that this was important for his self-respect and career, yet he seemed utterly unable to make the simple request that his boss treat him with dignity. This was puzzling until Norman told me that his mother, a perfectly coiffed alcoholic, would regularly fly into virulent fits of rage over seemingly insignificant incidents and then weep for hours with inconsolable grief. His father, a terminally self-involved State Department intelligence officer, who was prohibited by law to speak about what he did during the day, would walk out during his wife's histrionics and then return to sit silently in front of the TV, leaving Norman to absorb her wrath and despair. Early on he learned that confrontation was unacceptable and leaving was the best strategy.

This type of dynamic reveals that psychological insight alone is insufficient to bring forth a new way of being. While the origins of his aversion to conflict and the consequent passive behavior became clear to him, the understanding itself, though important, wasn't enough for Norman to change and take a stand for himself. While he knew that this was the best thing for him, his body simply wouldn't take the new action. This is where the practice of entering was critical for him to embody a new move that would enhance his self-respect and further his professional ambitions.

Equally curious was that Norman was anything but passive as a recreational basketball player. Playing informal pick-up games at his gym, he was extremely physical and had no qualms whatsoever about pushing people around on the court. This, of course, made others lean on him and he took spit-rattling hits by much larger players as a matter of course. On the court he radiated power and assertiveness; at the office you hardly noticed him. When I mentioned this incongruence between his life on the court and that at work, especially with his boss, Norman said that these were separate areas and had little connection with each other. "How does blocking a shot have anything to do with asking someone to treat me with more respect?" he asked.

"How could it not?" I responded.

I had Norman practice the entering movement that I described earlier. At first he simply performed the movement as if he were doing an exercise in the gym; he did it well in a bodily motor sense, but he wasn't making it relevant to his current dilemma at work.

Performing the movements without a "for the sake of what?" reduced it to a mindless physical workout.[9] When I brought this to Norman's attention he resisted, saying it was fruitless to add his commitment and intention to this physical activity. As we talked this through, his deep sense of despair about his boss became evident. Throughout the conversation he came to see that at the most fundamental level it wasn't so much about his boss changing, but Norman himself going through a transformation that could touch every part of his life; changing a lifetime of resignation to taking a stand for himself. What finally moved him was when he saw, in a moment of horror, that his behavior might be passed on to his sons. "I have three sons, nine to fourteen, and it's very important to me that they don't inherit this from me. I think they're okay so far, but already I can see some of this in my middle boy. If nothing else, it'll be worth it if they don't have to carry this weight." This galvanized Norman's commitment, and while it didn't make it smooth sailing, he put his shoulder to the wheel and worked hard.

As Norman practiced, he would visualize that the person coming toward him with an outstretched hand was his boss, and he'd speak the litany, "I do not accept how you relate to me. I feel mistreated and abused when you speak this way. I want you to stop and treat me with respect." As he practiced, he could see how his body would capitulate and he would lower his gaze and voice; yet as he continued over time he became stronger and more committed. At one point he asked for a meeting with his boss and had the conversation he had been putting off. "It was difficult," he reported, "but I believe he finally listened to what I was saying. I told him that if he didn't treat me differently I was going to move on."

Norman felt like he had accomplished something important for himself and this carried over to other areas of his life. He reported a growing feeling of confidence; his colleagues noted this as well. He continued the practices and he grew more skillful in taking a stand for himself. As it turned out, his boss's behavior didn't shift, and after bringing it up again, without a change from his boss, Norman asked for a transfer. His boss asked him to reconsider, but Norman said, "No, I've had enough." This was a loss for his team and the department, but they lauded his choice as a stand for his dignity.

Interestingly, after six successful months in his new role Norman took a leave of absence to be a stay-at-home dad with his three sons. When I saw him he was the happiest I'd ever seen him. He was his boy's baseball and basketball coach, he was running the affairs of the family, and working part-time helping his church in financial matters.

"What was unexpected," he said, "was that the practice of being in my body opened up new ways of being that I never dreamt of. Many things became possible that I would never let myself even imagine. Some say I'm more courageous, but for me it feels as if I'm just more open and willing to step into new things. I know that I'll reenter the workforce someday, but for right now I know I'm doing exactly what I'm meant to be doing, and that's a good feeling."

In the conversational domain, entering is making requests, assessments, declines, insists, and standards for behavior. While such communications are part of our everyday conversational patterns, it's not uncommon that they become unavailable to us in certain charged situations. As successful as Norman was, he was unable to make a direct request to his boss. He understood the necessity of doing so, but he didn't have the "body" to do it. As he built the "muscle" for engaging in the courageous conversations, he then saw other areas of his life that could also use this entering move. Norman is a classic example of learning a generative skill—entering, in this case—that becomes present and valuable in areas different than the one it was learned for.

Practices

- What are the conversations that you're avoiding and not entering into?

- When you think of having these conversations, what happens in your body? What sensations, moods, and thoughts occur? Where do you contract? What happens to your breath pattern? Does it speed up, do you hold it, where is it in your body?

- Choose a person or situation that you need to enter with but have been putting off. Before your daily solo practice and after you finish, speak your commitment to entering and engaging with this person or situation. Notice what happens in your body when you make this commitment.

- Have the conversation you need to have with this person. Notice what happens in your body as you're engaging with them. Are you relaxed, are you facing, are you contracting, did you make a clear request?

- Notice your mood, thinking, and feeling after the conversation. What was your learning?

- How does entering make you a more powerful leader?

Blending

An embodied commitment to *Collaboration and Partnership*

> To study the Way is to study the Self
>
> To study the Self is to forget the Self
>
> To Forget the Self is to be Awakened with All Things

Dogan, sixteenth-century Zen monk

To speak about blending as a domain of the body, it's useful to draw from the Japanese martial art, aikido. *Aikido* roughly translates as "the Way of Harmony with Energy." This seemingly paradoxical title for a martial art is more than a lofty ideal; centuries of sweat, blood, and trial have been spent by warriors learning that the principle of harmony is an effective martial response for success on the battlefield. Operationally this translates as blending with the energy of your attacker, joining with their force instead of struggling against them so you can use their momentum and power to resolve the conflict.

Morihei Ueshiba, the founder of aikido, who was a national living treasure of Japan and a renowned fighter and warrior, called his art *aikido* not out of sentimentality, but simply because the principle of *Aiki* works. He knew this to be so because in innumerable fights with larger opponents he walked away victorious without grievous injury to anyone. Being able to harmonize with his challengers' energy he was able to easily defeat them; moreover, many of them were so impressed by his skill and spiritual presence they remained as lifelong students. Aiki is not a soft, New Age idea that resides in hope, but a practical, sturdy, actionable principle of effectively coordinating with others.

165

In the martial arts context, blending, or the Aiki response, is extraordinarily powerful; its embodiment is what separates the master from the practitioner. Blending allows much smaller people the ability to handle the aggression of a larger, stronger opponent. Be clear that blending is not simply a "good idea" but a formidable way to deal with physical aggression in a skillful, effective manner. When a master of aikido blends with you, you suddenly feel as if you're tied to a volcano and a misstep can lead to serious injury, even death. Yet from the outside, the joining together looks effortless, almost dancelike; there's a total absence of collisions, clashes, or rough edges.

So daily fare in the aikido dojo, aside from learning the innumerable open-handed techniques and weapons systems, is the practice of bringing your energy into harmony with your partner's energy. Every encounter, every technique, every partner, however different, is being informed by Aiki: how to engage with a partner such that the practice promotes both balance and power—surely essential leadership principles.

While social and business leaders are not in the custom of being in physical confrontations, they have to daily take a stand on issues, fight for what is important, deal with negative incoming energy, and endlessly resolve conflicts. In the conversational spaces in which these actions take place, the principle of blending has a powerful application to our way of being as leaders.

To blend effectively one must act from a state of feeling and sensing; this requires us to live fully in our body. Blending asks us to be with someone in an extraordinarily intimate fierceness, to join with others in order to negotiate separateness, to transform aggression from discord to accord. This doesn't mean compliance, acquiescence, or submission but entering into the conflict with the commitment to see the world from the other's point of view and to legitimatize their perspective. This doesn't necessarily mean accepting their beliefs or values, but to accept that this is their worldview. It's not a soft-minded, passive surrender, but a disciplined, rigorous choice to put one's agenda aside to connect deeply not only with intentions, but what fuels those intentions.

We can see that from this point of view harmony, or *ai*, is not the simple-minded greeting card version of a modern couple walking hand in hand down a secluded beach into a mango-tinted sunset. The *kanji*, or character, of ai is two sides of a roof; and underneath this roof people are communing together. There is harmony among the people because the two sides of the roof come together strongly and forcefully and provide protection for those under it. It's not a weak-minded idea, but one of commitment, power, and strength.

The Samurai, the traditional Japanese warrior, in order to show proficiency in his art was graded on three things: *Shisei,* body alignment; *Kuzushi,* the ability to take an opponent's balance; and *Aiki,* the ability to harmonize with an opponent's energy. This system of grading reflects the importance of Aiki in dealing effectively with a partner or opponent in the martial context. We say this principle of Aiki is just as important for leaders in working effectively with partners, teammates, customers, employees, the marketplace, and competitors.

We must blend with someone from center. If we're in reaction, we won't feel our partner, their intentions or concerns. When we blend we learn to blend with what is, not how we think things should be. Blending brings us present with others and we meet them on equal footing. No wonder that the soldier and philosopher

Sir Francis Bacon said in the sixteenth century, "I know not why but the martial person is given to love."

At the heart of blending is *musubi,* which literally translates as "knot." The idea is to knot or tie your energy into the energy of your opponent or training partner. We practice musubi to become so connected to our partner, like two ropes joined by a knot, that we become one with her and are able to listen to her energy to reconcile the conflict, instead of fighting against her from a rigid position. Being with someone at the level of musubi means having an embodied understanding of that person's intentions, concerns, motivation, strengths, liabilities, fears, and commitments. This level of deep connection allows you to resolve conflicts and miscommunication in a skillful and respectful manner. Blending with someone's energy opens the opportunity for mutual success in which both parties feel that their concerns are listened to and respected. To tie into another's energy, we must extend toward him, put aside our self-consciousness, pretenses, and self-involvement, and pay attention to the other. When we're tied into someone in this way, we're able to build credibility, which in turn creates a bond that allows us to work together with maximum effectiveness and minimal effort.

When we tie into someone's energy, we're blending not only with her physical movements, but her essence—what she cares about, what she dreams of, what she's afraid of, what deeply matters to her. This is not simply an intellectual idea but a felt sense of someone, a way in which we allow ourselves to feel someone's being-ness, to somatically identify with the deepest part of the person. Blending is when we stand in the other person's shoes, see his perspective, engage with his interpretation of the world, feel what he feels, and then direct his energy toward partnership and collaboration. Blending is a deep listening that produces connection.

In the book, *A General Theory of Love*, Drs. Lewis, Amini, and Lannon report that six months before an infant will be able to stand up on its own, he or she can detect the most subtle changes in the emotional responsiveness of a caregiver. As human beings we seek a limbic resonance, "a symphony of mutual exchange and internal adaptation whereby two mammals become attuned to each other's inner states."[10] We are biologically designed to tune in to those around us, always evaluating the depth and quality of connectedness with others. This thrust toward connection is factory loaded; it comes with being a human being. It's part of our genetic code and spiritual inheritance to join with others for belonging, support, security, reciprocity, and love. In our normal conversation we often refer to this as "feeling someone"—"He feels sad" or "She feels distant" or "She feels disengaged" or "He's upset"—having a sense of someone or a situation that lives beyond the scope of words. All of us have an innate capacity and desire (that is often socialized out of us) to blend with others so we can participate and engage with them at the deepest level possible. In the Leadership Dojo, we practice blending so we can better serve others.

In nearly four decades of working with people I've seen that this level of connection has more impact in strengthening relationships and building trust than anything else. I don't know how to explain it, but I've consistently seen that blending at this deep emotional level increases partnership, innovation, and team alignment. Blending is in our biological nature as a powerful, innate desire to connect and to be understood. When William James, the renowned American psychologist, said, "The deepest human need is to be appreciated," he wasn't making a casual heart-warming statement to soothe. Through decades of studying people, he saw the core emotional need we have is for our concerns and needs to be seen and acknowledged. Marianne Bentzen, in her groundbreaking book *The Body Self in Psychotherapy: A Psychomotoric Approach to Developmental Psychology,* systematically shows that the need for connection is the fundamental human driving force and in doing so represents a major departure from how psychology has traditionally defined humanity. These are the ways we speak about blending in the relationship and conversational domains.[11]

As the final principle in the Leadership Presence, blending allows us to connect with others so we can best join and partner with them.

We do specific exercises and movements that train this quality as an embodied response to incoming energy. Remember that the other four principles—centering, facing, extending, entering—precede blending. Also remember that they are like notes that comprise a chord, all happening simultaneously.

Practices

- Have a partner move toward you with his or her arm outstretched toward your chest, as we did in the previous exercises. As your partner moves in your direction, embody the first four principles and then turn from center and move with him in the direction he's going. Walk side by side with him in the direction he's going, at his rhythm, at his speed, in his gait. Feel what it's like to be in his shoes, inhabit his view of the world, be in his skin. Though this might seem like a strange idea, keep in mind that this way of sensing and feeling is at

the core of how we listen deeply to others. True, you wouldn't necessarily do this with someone in the office, but our claim is that by
practicing this somatically you build the sensibility and skill to blend
with someone in their conversational space.

Here's a practice we do in aikido that's called the "basic blend," a practice so important we begin every class with it.

- Put your right foot forward and extend your right arm waist high,
  palm down in the direction of your partner. Your partner will have
  her left foot forward and she'll grab your right wrist with her left
  hand palm down. Have your partner push into you, and you push
  back defensively, as if your only choice is to confront and fight with
  her. Notice what that feels like and what moods, emotions, stories,
  and sensations it brings up.

- Now as your partner pushes toward you, collapse your arm and let
  her overrun you, like you're a victim and have no power or accountability for what's occurring. Notice what that feels like and what
  moods, emotions, stories, and sensations it brings up.

- Now, after embodying the first four principles—centering, facing, extending, entering—you'll move next to your partner as she
  pushes forward, turn from center, and blend with the flow of energy
  and intention in her grab. See what she's looking at, the direction
  she's moving, her speed, balance, force, and so on. Simply said:
  Feel your partner. Tie into those you're leading. Notice what blending feels like and what moods, emotions, stories, and sensations it
  generates.

By doing this as a feeling and sensing practice in order to tie into your partner's energy, and not simply as a motor exercise, you learn to blend with someone in the conversational space.

The trajectory of Susan's professional career reflects the importance of blending in leadership positions.

Susan is an intelligent, charming woman in her late thirties who's an emerging leader in her company as a marketing executive. She has raven-black hair and a blazing smile, but above the bridge of her nose her eyes are frozen. Her pupils are like chips of blue ice embedded in a forehead of tiny furrows. Susan talks team but acts tyrant. She speaks excitedly about the importance of collaboration; "Everyone's opinion counts," she will say. Or, "I want us to reach agreement through consensus." But at the end of the day, she doesn't listen to others, and it's her ideas that she pushes through. The split in her face mirrors the split between what she says and what she does. Susan's somatic structure prohibits her from blending and partnering with others.

The way she runs meetings brings this contradiction to the foreground. She warmly welcomes everyone, praises the team, puts forward the meeting agenda, speaks her ideas, and then lavishly invites everyone to join in "so we can synergistically come up with the best strategy and action plan." She then lights up the room with her scorching smile and positions her pad and pen expectantly. Things proceed evenly until an idea different than hers begins to gather momentum. Up to this point everything Susan had asked for from her team was occurring—engaged participation, honoring others, and respect for ideas—yet she was becoming more and more tense.

She would shake her head dismissively, "I think what we really ought to do is ..." and then reiterate her ideas in a slightly different form, her eyes hardening a notch, her smile turning into a snarl. When a bright, well-groomed fellow strengthened his own position, she held up her hand up in a stop position with her head slightly angled away, "As I said, if we want to accomplish this we need to . . ." and again pitched her idea in a tone that told you she wasn't inviting a vote. And so the meeting went.

A gloom settled in the room, and everyone slowly sank back studying their fingernails or looking blankly at the air vents. They were gone; bodies parked in chairs with no one home, missing in action. Susan declared who was going to do what and triumphantly ended the meeting. There was a palpable sense of resignation as the team filed out of the room. When she and I debriefed the meeting she entirely missed what had happened.

"Everyone put their ideas on the table and we all talked them over and then came to a course of action. Sure we had some disagreements but that's part of the process," she explained.

When I confronted her with what I saw, she made the same moves with me as she did with her team—she became closed to how I saw the meeting. She was locked inside her self-imposed walls, defending her position as if her very life depended on it. When I told her that the kind of feedback I was giving her was what she had asked for, and that her defensiveness only worked against her, she came up short, desperate, the smile gone.

Susan is the youngest child of a highly educated professional family who held intellectual prowess as a virtue and also as a battering ram on whoever didn't measure up. The training ground was family meals where debating social and political issues was a blood sport. Her father, an orthopedic surgeon, would disappear in a sour mood of condescension if one of the children didn't meet his intellectual standards, which was all the time; her mother, a college professor, would unabashedly compete with Susan, telling her not to interrupt and then interrupted her with an ever-increasing volume until she would be red-faced and shouting, viciously belittling her. The older brother was a corporate lawyer, stabbing his finger toward the others, attempting to out-shout the mother. The other brother, the dean of a prestigious liberal arts university, would slowly fade into the background to the contempt of his brother and parents.

In this verbal brawl, Susan learned that acceptance came with staying in the ring, taking the punches, and defending her ideas to the end. Disengagement meant dismissal, not just of her ideas, but also of her as a person. Emotional responses like sadness or hurt represented weakness, as did simply being an informed listener, and both would provoke the ire of the family, turning them into a pack of mad dogs competing for the kill. She remembered the moment when she decided that it was better to go down fighting than to move off her position.

"At one point I was so frustrated I began to cry, and my mother began to mimic me in a sarcastic tone and my older brother joined her. My father sat staring at me, his silence as dense as the sound in a mineshaft. He seemed to say, 'Susan, if you don't learn to stand and fight for yourself you'll be a loser forever. You can't expect to be somebody if you go around whimpering.' And then he pushed himself away from the table and walked away. It was a turning point. I saw that to gain acceptance and respect in this family, especially as the only daughter, I had to be tough; I had to be smart and never show weakness, never give in. It wouldn't work for me to acquiesce like my other brother either. Collaboration or coming together over an idea was not the game that paid off. From that point on, I promised myself that I would never let my emotions show and I wouldn't stop fighting. I would prove to them that I was in control of myself and I wouldn't let them get the best of me. My father was different toward me when I did this, more friendly though I can't say he was ever really warm. But surely more accepting and more kind in his own way. It was clear that this was the way to gain his approval."

In this decision Susan became a fortress, a self-created Alamo in which surrender or opening wasn't an option. Being tough and holding her position at all costs was her ticket to belonging. At the same time her father required that she maintain her femininity and act the role of the gracious host. Her unrelenting smile and southern belle persona were her token gestures of congeniality, but her eyes gave away the controlling, unforgiving competitor. She had learned enough management techniques to talk the right talk, but it only thinly covered the layer of rigidity and fear that was under her false front of conviviality.

Susan's somatic rigidity in her frozen eyes, constricted breath, and iron-clad shoulders compelled her into defending and fighting when she was challenged or when someone disagreed with her. This created an identity of someone who was uncaring and manipulative, who didn't listen or care about what others thought. Because of this she was mistrusted and people moved away from her. Her career was being jeopardized and she was beginning to suffer because of it; this was the pain point that made her seek out a different way. She sincerely cared about being different, but the behavior was deeply embodied in her. It wasn't sufficient for her to cognitively "know" about this automatic reaction, she had to change the protective covering in her body that had become her default to this conditioned tendency. Susan was aware enough to cognitively know that what she was doing wasn't working, but she was so deeply trapped in it that she didn't know a way out.

My focus with Susan was to build a somatic sensibility through the practices of centering, facing, extending, and entering so she could become more aware of how she reflexively organized herself toward defending; this would open new choices and practices for her. This ground had to be established before she could build the body to blend and partner with others. I also began by working on the armoring around her eyes, face, and shoulders.[12]

I began by teaching her how she could relax her eye and face muscles. Though her eyes were strikingly clear, they were also hard and lacked warmth, making it difficult to contact her through her gaze. She looked like she was frozen in a moment of fright, much like the startled look in the eyes of a deer when caught unexpectedly in the glare of headlights. She described her vision as looking down a long tunnel; without flexibility in her eyes there was no possibility for lateral movement or peripheral vision. To the untrained person, this might give the impression of being focused, but in fact the contraction in her pupils and eyes were transferred to her brain through the optic nerve and then precipitated through her central nervous system as a low-grade chronic tension in her entire body. In addition, this "look" intimidated people, making them cautious in her presence.

I asked her to do movements with her eyes that stretched the muscles that governed eye movement. I would have her visually follow my finger as I made movements in circles, left and right, and figure eights. While she did this she engaged in a breath pattern that was rhythmic and deep. As her eyes began to relax, they appeared softer and more available. Her smile took on a more authentic countenance and her breath dropped from high and rapid in her chest to deep in her lower abdomen.

I also showed her exercises she could do to release the tension in her neck and shoulder girdle. I did deep tissue bodywork on these areas to help relieve the chronic holding. The muscles along her spine from her skull to her tailbone were like long ropes of steel. The entire musculature in her upper body was working overtime to hold her upright. She was in a constant struggle against gravity, as if she were afraid to let herself down, to feel the ground and be among people. Susan was chronically steeling herself against some perceived attack. This was the way she had learned to organize herself when her family gathered, and over time it had become part of her. Although she was years away from the family table, her body was still vigilant for assault and was coiled to counter-attack. Even though she "knew" this, the somatic organization was so fixed at this point that it didn't allow her to take a different path of action. This shape of "ready to fight" that Susan lived in had to be dismantled for her to fulfill on her aspirations as a person and a leader. For her to blend with others and build strong partnerships and alliances she needed a new body, a body that was both flexible and strong, a body that could take a strong stand for something but at the same time could listen to others and build trust with them.

As she was changing through these practices, another phenomena began to occur that is common in this kind of transformation. When the armoring around Susan's eyes and upper body began to dissolve, a feeling of panic quickly displaced the initial sense of wonder at how pleasantly different she felt.

"I feel too vulnerable this way. I don't know if I'd be able to protect myself and I'm not sure that I'm making sense to people. How do I look? Do I look funny?" she asked anxiously after one of our sessions.

When I asked her to return to her sensations, and not her judgments and fear, she reported that she felt "warm and relaxed, a sense of being bigger."

"What's scary about that?"

"It's just that I feel so different, I'm not sure of myself this way. It's a feeling of vulnerability, like I could be taken advantage of, I wouldn't be able to protect myself."

"Who do you need to protect yourself from?"

"I know it doesn't make sense. It's just how I feel. Do you think I'll be okay like this?"

It was a poignant moment and one that many people experience when the armoring that has organized them for so long begins to dissolve. Because our worldview is so intimately connected to our somatic structure, a feeling of either well-being or terror will often accompany this disorganization and subsequent reorganization. In the transition from one body to another, it's as if our very existence, our sense of self, is in question and it's necessary that we engage in a new worldview. For some this is good news and for others it's a nightmare; and there are many shades that lie between.

Practice

Open your eyes wide, raise your shoulders about an inch, and bite down on your teeth while you smile and move your breath into your chest. If you hold this posture long enough you'll begin to see how it influences your mood, thinking, and what is possible and not possible in terms of how you behave and how you're limited in making contact with others. Ask someone what opinions come to them when they see you in this particular somatic organization. The shape you're now taking will also shape your identity. That is, the way people see you and whether or not they identify you as someone they can trust and partner with. This was the way Susan had been organizing herself since adolescence.

What you just did in this practice will feel either comfortable or uncomfortable, depending upon how you've been shaping yourself up to this point in your life. While this may seem exaggerated to you, it is in no way an unusual pattern of somatic organization. This shape, like all shapes we hold ourselves in, brings forth a reality or a certain perception of the world. Imagine that you've been in this shape for most of your life. Now slowly dismantle it by relaxing your eyes, lowering your shoulders, letting the mouth and jaw relax, and breathing lower in your abdomen. If you did this and paid attention to the shifts you went through, you can get a sense of the changes you would go through as your body reorganizes into a new shape. A whole new world of self, others, and the environment opens.

This is the change Susan went through as she moved from a body that was armored and defended to one that was open and receptive. At each stage of transformation she was reassured that this was part of the path that took her toward fulfilling her embodied leadership potential. A major aspect of that reassurance was that she saw how people were different around her; they more readily shared their ideas, they were more genuinely open to her ideas, her team grew in unity and alignment and produced far better results than ever before, and her direct reports ranked high satisfaction in the workplace that she created.

As Susan continued her work in the Leadership Dojo, she became literate with how she could organize herself in a relaxed but alert manner. Over time she became more at ease with her changes and was able to let others in more easily. Her team members began to comment that she seemed "more relaxed and wasn't trying so hard." When she would start to react and go into her fighting mode, she could now feel what that was like in her body and she was able to return to center more quickly. When she was overtaken by her reactive mode, she could now identify what was occurring: "I can feel a heat rising in me, I bite down on my teeth and whoever is in front of me looks like they're a long ways away, down at the end of long tunnel." Because she could now identify how her body was organized to fight, she was less of a victim to it, and she could settle into herself and listen to another person's point of view instead of defending her own.

Having established this ground, even if it was different than her own, Susan could now tolerate blending with and listening deeply to others. She could energetically feel into others and gain a sense of their mood, what moved them, what threw them off, what they cared about, when they were no longer paying attention. It became apparent that this new behavior was very attractive to her team. They had more fun together and were far more productive. Her team could see that she was different and they began to trust that she would listen to their ideas and that she was sincere when she said she wanted everyone's participation.

"I would never have guessed that being closer to others like this would actually make me feel safer. And you know I'm actually curious and interested in the people on my team now. I like them and am so glad we're working together." Susan also began to see that by listening and blending she began to hear her team's ideas and saw that what they had to offer genuinely contributed to the enterprise. Over time she began to see that much of her job had to do with growing and developing her people and not competing with them. This cut down on both her stress and her workload, and she found herself more fulfilled in her leadership role. Years later I heard from her and she said she was happily married with a young daughter. In her note she said, "My little girl is learning how to have fun at the dinner table."

Remember that blending is not necessarily agreeing with someone or submitting to what they want. Blending is the skill of listening deeply to the concerns of others and then making the most appropriate moves that take the action forward. There are, of course, books written on the tips and techniques of communication skills that promise if you say things like "That's very interesting," or "Tell me more," or "I can see why you'd feel that way," or if you say the person's name before each sentence you'll build trust and intimacy and defuse conflict. This simple-minded approach to leadership trivializes our ability to distinguish between what's genuine and what's insincere. Furthermore it sets us up to be seen as superficial and inauthentic. It's only when we truly care about others and are genuinely curious about what matters to them that the possibilities

181

of strong partnerships and sustainable relationships come to life. This way of being comes from a living, centered presence, which in turn is built on embodied practices. Parroting slogans and mouthing set phrases only undermine the depth of connection that's possible for us.

Blending informs us *how* to take the action. Sometimes it may mean raising your voice and being forceful, other times it may mean being quiet, moving closer to the person, moving further away, or declining the conversation altogether. It's a deep sense of the right move, almost an instinct, that allows you to tie into the energy of your partner to move with her in an effective manner. Blending with a situation or person, we are no longer struggling against them, and this allows us to be in touch with the essential nature of the relationship.

Practices

- Reflect on your ability to blend with others. Is it an in-place embodied skill, or do you have difficulty blending? Is it context specific, that is, do you blend well in some situations and not in others?

- Ask someone who knows you to give you an assessment about your ability to blend.

- Reflect on the cost to you of not blending in certain relationships and/or situations.

- Sit or stand in a centered stance in front of some aspect of nature—a tree, pond, rose bush, mountain, valley—and blend with its essence. Using both your synaesthesia and imagination, actually be the thing you're blending with. See it as a way to understand the essence of that part of nature. What did you notice in sensation, mood, emotion, or story? What do you see possible in blending?

- Do the same practice above but in a public place such as a mall, a park, or a coffee shop and pick someone to blend with. Center, face, extend, enter, and blend with the essence of this person. What is the mood, emotion, sensation, or story that emerges? Do not be concerned if it's true or not; it's only you practicing blending. What do you notice about yourself? What have you learned?

- With whom would you like to build a partnership? How can you better blend and listen to him or her to enhance this partnership. Practice doing this in real time and notice what happens in your mood, emotion, sensation, or story. What was your learning?

- How does blending make you a better leader?

EXAMPLES OF LEADERSHIP PRESENCE

A Leadership Presence is a fundamental and core aspect of one's power. It's not just a good idea or a fashionable homily, but rather a living presence we can embody through practice. It's important to remember that though we have divided it into five steps, when we embody them they all happen simultaneously, like five notes producing a chord. Consider the aikido master who, when confronted by an opponent, will embody these five principles in a moment of skillful action. This is the leader who embodies skillful action, pragmatic wisdom, and grounded compassion.

Let me give you two examples of a Leadership Presence. The first comes from the martial arts and the second from the conversational, relationship space. The martial perspective can make the distinctions of the Leadership Presence easily understandable and transferable to other domains, even though most people do not get into physical confrontations.

Sarah's been training in the martial arts for the past fifteen years. In the early years she did some competing, but recently she's been training to keep her skills sharp, maintain her fitness, and stay close to the dojo community who comprise her core friendships. She's not particularly big or strong, but she's confident in her body and she understands physical confrontation.

One evening Sarah leaves work after dark and as she enters the parking garage two men walk toward her. She makes a wide berth around them, but they angle toward her, making catcalls.

Centering.   Sarah feels the rush of adrenaline in her body and immediately straightens and settles herself. She breathes deep in her belly, extends her energy, and opens her peripheral vision. She becomes present in her mind/body and also to the environment. She notices the men are big, drunk but not yet stumbling, and they continue to move steadily toward her. She also notes that there's no one else around.

Facing.   Since there's no easy exit and she knows she can't outrun them she turns toward them and assumes a relaxed but alert stance that she knows from her martial training. Her stance embodies commitment, balance, and power. They make some comments about her that indicate they notice her present demeanor but still move toward her.

Extending.   She extends her attention toward them and assesses that they probably have no formal martial training, their drinking has slowed their reflexes, but they're big and emboldened by each other. Their behavior and dress tell her they're probably not street criminals, but they are potentially dangerous nonetheless.

Entering.   They continue to move toward her and she holds up one hand and in a calm voice says, "Stop, that's close enough." For a moment they stop and then one of them takes out a cigarette and says, "How about lighting me up?" They both laugh. She puts up her hand again, takes a step forward, and speaks with composed force, "I don't have a light. Back off."

Blending.   A frozen tableau in the dimly lit garage of two men and a woman facing each other: her hand up, the men caught in a moral crossroads. Then one steps forward and awkwardly reaches out. "It's okay honey, don't worry," he slurs. Immediately and without hesitation she does a quick turning movement, ending up behind him, holding her cell phone up, her finger on the send button, "You guys look like you might need some help. Here I'll dial 911. Remember, don't drink and drive!" Her voice is penetrating and echoing in the underground labyrinth. She wheels around and strides confidently off. They appear dumbfounded for a moment and then go in the opposite direction.

Here's an example of centering, facing, extending, entering, and blending in the organizational domain.

As a vice president and confidante to the CEO, Roger has advised him in a speech he's to deliver to the company. When they meet a few minutes before the meeting, the CEO tells Roger that he feels ill and can't go on. He asks Roger to stand in for him and give the speech.

Centering. Roger feels a knot forming in his stomach and his pulse quickening. He recognizes the anxious voices concerning this sudden change of events that advise he look for a way out. He straightens his belt buckle, which is his way of reminding himself to drop his attention and his breath to his center of gravity. He settles his weight into his chair and feels his feet solidly on the floor. From this stance he reminds himself how he's created trust with the CEO for him to make this request. He now feels present to move forward.

Facing. Roger faces what's ahead of him by reviewing who will be there, what has to be accomplished, the main points of the speech he helped craft, and the condition of the CEO. He also faces that he's nervous and instead of trying to push it away he accepts it as natural to the sudden change of events and that it's simply energy that is present to help him to do the job.

Extending. Roger asks the CEO, "At the completion of this speech what do you want to accomplish?" When the CEO tells him his conditions of success, Roger asks a few clarifying questions and then feels he fully embodies what is required of him. Roger assures the CEO that he'll deliver.

Entering.   Roger steps confidently onto the stage and immediately extends toward the audience. He connects personally with as many of them as he can. His energetic presence reaches into the entire room. He's relaxed and fully engaged.

Blending.   Embodying the fully committed presence of a leader, Roger addresses the group's concerns: From the CEO being ill, to being asked to deliver the speech, to requesting that everyone commit to fulfill on this year's goals, to engage in a spirit of unity, to keep their overall mission in view, and thanking and acknowledging them for what they've accomplished. The few times he stumbles over the slides in the presentation, he good-naturedly makes fun of himself and draws laughs from the audience.

NOTES

One: We Are All Leaders

1. Marlin Company Poll. "Attitudes in the American Workplace." May–June 2004. Retrieved January 2007 from http://www.themarlincompany.com/poll/media.htm

Two: The Cultivation of the Self

1. Smith, Page. *A New Age Begins: A Peoples' History of the American Revolution.* New York: Penguin Books, 1989.

2. Brookhiser, Richard. *Founding Father.* New York: Free Press, 1996, p. 111.

3. Fromm, Eric. *On Disobedience and Other Essays.* New York: Seabury, 1981.

4. For further insight into the concept of *shugyo,* I highly recommend *Aikido and the Harmony of Nature* (Boston: Shambhala, 1993), by Mitsugi Saotome Sensei. Saotome Sensei is my aikido teacher, and many of the ideas in this chapter as well as in Chapter Three have been fleshed out through innumerable conversations with him. I owe him a deep debt of gratitude for his influence and guiding hand.

Three: The Place of Awakening

1. In my book *Holding the Center,* there are additional distinctions about the sensibility of Dojo Learning: in the essay "Place of Awakening" (p. 25) and in the essay "Teachership" (p. 39).

Four: You Are What You Practice

1. *The Ellen DeGeneres Show,* July 8, 2004.
2. Leonard, George. *Mastery: The Keys to Success and Long-Term Fulfillment.* New York: Plume Books, 1992.
3. Packer, George. "Letter from Baghdad, War after War." *New Yorker,* November 24, 2003, p. 62.

Five: The Body of a Leader

1. Barlow, J. P. "A Declaration of the Independence of Cyberspace." February 8, 1996. Retrieved 2006 from http://homes.eff.org/~barlow/ Declaration-Final.html
2. In conversation with the poet David Whyte.
3. While this word is derived from ancient Greek, Thomas Hanna, Ph.D, brought it into contemporary conversation. Thomas Hanna was the chair of my Ph.D. dissertation and a strong influence on my studies of somatics. I recommend his books to those further interested in the art and science of somatics: *Somatics: Reawakening the Mind's Control of Movement, Flexibility, and Health* (Cambridge, MA: Da Capo Press, 2004); *The Body of Life: Creating New Pathways for Sensory Awareness and Fluid Movement* (Rochester, NY: Healing Arts Press, 1993); and *Bodies in Revolt: A Primer in Somatic Thinking* (Novato, CA: Freeperson Press, 1985).

4. Gladwell, Malcolm. "The Naked Face." *New Yorker,* August 5, 2002, p. 47.

5. Throughout this book, I refer to commitments made in language. This notion of language as an embodied commitment derives from the work of Fernando Flores, Ph.D. Throughout most of the 1990s, I worked closely with Dr. Flores, consulting with organizations in North America, the United Kingdom, Mexico, and South America. His work with language as action is truly revolutionary and has positively affected how countless leaders and managers run their companies. He is currently a Senator in Chile; for the interested reader, I recommend these books: *Building Trust: In Business, Politics, Relationships, and Life* (Oxford: Oxford University Press, 2003); *Understanding Computers and Cognition: A New Foundation for Design* (Boston: Addison-Wesley Professional); and *Disclosing New Worlds: Entrepreneurship, Democratic Action, and the Cultivation of Solidarity* (with Hubert L. Dreyfus and Charles Spinosa; Cambridge, MA: MIT Press, 1999).

6. Havel, Vaclav et al. *The Power of the Powerless.* London: Hutchinson, 1985, p. 38.

Six: Leadership Presence

1. Mehrabian, Albert. *Silent Messages.* Belmont, CA: Wadsworth, 1971.

2. For an additional perspective on centering, read "Center: The Unity of Action and Being" in my book *Holding The Center: Sanctuary in a Time of Confusion* (p. 95), as well as in *The Anatomy of Change* (p. 79).

3. The ability to face directly into the world makes us both more vulnerable and more powerful. When mammals of the same species fight and one becomes dominant, the other will roll over on its back and present its exposed underbelly to signal that it recognizes the

other as dominant. For most species, this ends the fight, and they both take their appropriate place in the hierarchy of the pack. The exposing of one's belly, or ventral side, is called an "appeasement cue" in that it signals one's vulnerability to the other's dominance and it ends a cycle of aggression. Consider that we, as humans, walk around with our soft underbelly continually exposed to others. Rationally, of course, we do not think we're in danger by exposing our front, nor do we rationally think that we're signaling others that they are dominant so they can back off. After hundreds of thousands of years of biologically living in this response, how does it occur under the rational mind as we face people on a daily basis? Deep within our nervous system how do we process these ancient signals? Are our bodies saying to each other "I'm vulnerable to you," "I'm strong enough to show my vulnerability," "I need to struggle with you since we are both open and vulnerable," or "I need to comply and acquiesce since we are both open and vulnerable"? There is no explicit biological signal that we wish either to withdraw from the fight or continue in it. We can speculate that this constant exposing of one's vulnerability, without a clear appeasement cue, may produce a compensatory protective mechanism that results in either extreme of projecting toughness and defensiveness as a way of protection or projecting a meekness and contraction as a preemptive move signaling the other not to be aggressive. A Leadership Presence, which includes the attribute of facing, must necessarily take into account that the way we comport ourselves in regards to facing may be deeply influenced by the relatively new capacity for standing that we have as *Homo sapiens*. In other words, can we have greater choice over our automatic response of fear, whether it's acted out in aggression or acquiescence, by the way we comport ourselves?

4. In their article "The Neuroscience of Leadership" in *Strategy+Business*, David Rock and Jeffrey Schwartz make a compelling scientific

argument that how and what we pay attention to is critical in learning and change. Those readers who would like to delve deeper into how science has grounded the importance of the attention in leadership, success, and fulfillment can refer to *A User's Guide to the Brain: Perception, Attention, and the Four Theatres of the Brain* (New York: Pantheon, 2001); *The Mind and The Brain: Neuroplasticity and the Power of Mental Force* (New York: Regan Books, 2002); "Quantum Physics in Neuroscience and Psychology: A Neurophysical Model of the Mind-Brain Interaction," *Philosophical Transactions of the Royal Society B: Biological Sciences* 360:1458, June 29, 2005.)

5. See my book *The Anatomy of Change*, in the chapter "Living in the Body" (p. 59), where I go into more detail on the attention as a requisite for fulfillment and mastery.

6. Chuang Tzu. "Cutting Up an Oxen," quoted by Thomas Merton in *The Way of Chuang Tzu*. New York: New Directions Books, 1969, pp. 45–47.

7. I speak about the Organ of Attention and its importance in *The Anatomy of Change.*

8. For more about *irimi* refer to my books, *The Anatomy of Change* (p. 90) and *Holding the Center* (p. 87/Saotome Sensei as well).

9. In *Holding the Center* (p.118), I speak about athletes and performers who fall in the trap of being in a performing body. They can do extraordinary things physically, but it doesn't translate into other areas of their life. We can readily see that being a high-level athlete or performer doesn't automatically mean you'll be a strong performer off the playing field; drug abuse, social aggression, and failed relationships are cases in point. However, the point I continually emphasize is that through practices, intention, and narratives we can build a "body" that excels in leadership. This requires connecting one's intention and purpose to the activity. This returns us to the stonecutter's story in

which the power lies in keeping the "cathedral" in mind while we do the activity. This is what puts our vision in the muscle and how we train new skills.

10. Lewis, Thomas, Fari Amini, and Richard Lannon. *A General Theory of Love.* New York: Vintage, 2001.

11. Bentzen, Marianne, Erik Jarles, and Peter Levine. *The Body Self in Psychotherapy: A Psychomotric Approach to Developmental Psychology.* New York: Crossroads, 1994.

12. Armoring is a distinction developed by Wilhelm Reich, a German psychiatrist and student of Freud's. Reich began to see that many of his clients weren't responsive to Freud's "talking cure." Through rigorous observation of his patients he posited that the neurosis lived in their tissues, and it was necessary to work directly with the body to free the person from their conditioning and what ailed them. Through touch, gestures, movement, and breath patterns he began to work directly on the tissues of his clients with great success. He claimed that over time it was possible to release the chronic holding in the body—the "armoring"—and to regain emotional balance and mental clarity. He left a rich and dense body of work that can be reviewed in *The Collected Works of Wilhelm Reich.*